AN INTRODUCTION TO *ECO-ETHICA*

Tomonobu Imamichi

Translated by
Judy Wakabayashi

UNIVERSITY PRESS OF AMERICA,® INC.
Lanham • Boulder • New York • Toronto • Plymouth, UK

Copyright © 2009 by **University Press of America,**® **Inc.**

4501 Forbes Boulevard
Suite 200
Lanham, Maryland 20706
UPA Acquisitions Department (301) 459-3366

Estover Road
Plymouth PL6 7PY
United Kingdom

All rights reserved. Printed in the United States of America British Library Cataloging in Publication Information Available

Library of Congress Control Number: 2009925435
ISBN: 978-0-7618-4554-6 (paperback : alk. paper)
eISBN: 978-0-7618-4555-3

∞™ The paper used in this publication meets the minimum requirements of American National Standard for Information Sciences—Permanence of Paper for Printed Library Materials, ANSI Z39.48-1992

Contents

Preface   v

Preface to English edition   xi

1. Preliminary Thoughts on the Essence of *Eco-ethica*   1
   Why ethics now?
      The contrary opposition between death and virtue
      The unprecedented ethical issues raised by new technology

2. Reinstating Ethics   15
      Our responsibility toward nature and things
      Changes affecting the human habitat
      Ethics for living *well*
      Why is ethics being forgotten?
      Turning into skilled animals
      Eco-ethica in our day-to-day lives

3. A New Virtue Ethics   33
      Virtues as the specific manifestation of an ethical system
      The history of creating virtues
      The creation of new virtues

4. Morals and Logic   53
      The Japanese moral consciousness
      The technology-mediated environment and changes in moral consciousness
      The logical structure of action
      Technological abstraction—a new form of abstraction

Self-regulation of technology and of humans
   The mythos of fire

5 **Human Beings and Nature** 75
   The position of human beings in primordial nature
   Nature and the technology-mediated environment
   Learning from nature

Invitees to the International Symposium on Eco-ethica 93

Index 95

Preface

THE FIRST BOOK ON *ECO-ETHICA*

This book is about a new ethics demanded by the times that lie ahead of us. Known as *eco-ethica* (a word whose origins will be explained in Chapter 1), this is a new ethics for a new dimension of human life. *Eco-ethica* is the name of a discipline that I proposed in the mid-1960s and that gained international recognition in the 1970s. Nowadays an international journal of philosophy[1] is published annually by the research institute of which I am director. Containing first-rate papers on *eco-ethica* by internationally renowned contributors, this journal has attracted attention in various quarters around the world. Since its goal is to foster international collaborative studies, the papers are written in European languages, so unfortunately *eco-ethica* is not yet sufficiently well known in Japan, its country of origin. This year, the tenth anniversary of the International Symposium on Eco-ethica that is held annually in Japan, it occurred to me to publish a scholarly yet accessible introduction to *eco-ethica*. Since I am the sole author, this work presents my own views, rather than reporting on joint research. I have reproduced the transcripts of selected lectures that I have given at several universities and workshops over the past few years. Although the talks were lectures, they are in spoken language, making this an easy read for a book on philosophy. To help readers follow the main arguments, I have omitted detailed explanations, leaving out supplementary material such as comments added during the lectures in the form of handouts

---

[1] *Revue Internationale de Philosophie Moderne.* ISSN 0915-1818. Published by the Centre International pour Étude Comparée de Philosophie et d'Esthètique, Shiozaki Building, 2-7-1, Hirakawa-cho, Chiyoda-ku, Tokyo.

or notes on the blackboard. Readers interested in a more in-depth discussion are referred to my papers in the above-mentioned journal. Despite these omissions, I believe the book presents an innovative argument that maintains high academic standards in the presentation of its findings.

THE STRATIFICATION OF THE ETHICAL SUBJECT

It would not be farfetched to describe *eco-ethica* as a bid to revolutionize ethics, but just why is such a provocative attempt needed at this point in time? The answer that immediately springs to mind is the broadening of the range of actions in the twentieth century, which witnessed the development of science and technology. In other words, because technology as a means has transmogrified into science and technology, it has expanded its scope and capabilities, with a concomitant broadening in the range—and impact—of technological actions, thereby giving rise to a need for *responsibility* as a virtue. In conjunction with this, technological means have moved out of the hands of individuals, instead becoming owned by groups and, in particular, falling under the reins of state power. Just think of the difference between candles and electricity, between the spear and nuclear weapons.

Such developments make it imperative to reflect on an issue that has been largely overlooked in the past—i.e., group ethics, particularly on the part of companies and governments. One of the distinctive features of *eco-ethica* lies in the fact that it explores not just individuals, but also organizations, as ethical subjects. The threat of nosism on the part of organizations, as distinct from the threat posed by egoism in individuals, lies in the fact that organizations entice people with their fine-sounding names; moreover, despite the fact that organizations have powerful means in their control, the locus of responsibility remains unclear. Wars make people question whether in such situations politics trumps morality and the state tolerates a moratorium on morality. What rationale can be given for the primacy of morality in relation to such issues of concern to people, and what steps should be taken to ensure its primacy? In this way the stratification of the ethical subject raises a whole raft of new issues.

THE STRATIFICATION OF THE ETHICAL OBJECT

While remaining utilitarian in essence, science and technology have, since around the sixties, moved beyond this dimension to constitute a huge environment that I refer to as *conjunction technologique* (the technology-mediated environment). This has become established alongside nature as a new human environment, evoking expectations of an ethics that differs from the behavioral norms established when our environment consisted solely of nature. In the everyday act of speaking, for instance, our actual neighbours are in close physical proximity to us, but with the technology-mediated environment people in far-flung corners of the globe become our neighbours via the telephone. So inadvertently dialing a wrong number or getting the time zone wrong means you end up waking a complete stranger in the middle of the night, far off in some foreign country. This not only creates a need for *accuracy* as a virtue, but also indicates that the broadening of ethics beyond a specific minority of visible neighbours to an unspecified majority of invisible and unknown neighbours transcends the limits of person-to-person ethics to encompass the entire human race alive at any particular time. And matters don't stop there. Our ethical responsibilities to the next generation and future unborn generations entail creating a fine culture if that is within our powers, passing our culture on, and preserving a healthy balance in nature.

The technology-mediated environment is also encroaching on nature, transforming it on a massive scale, so we need to consider behavioral norms in relation to nature from an ethical perspective. In this way ethics must transcend interpersonal ethics to also encompass an ethics toward things. An awareness of ourselves not as subjugators of nature but merely as beings entrusted with its stewardship will lead to a new *humility*. And if an ethics toward things is necessary, the fact that objects have cultural and technological outcomes means that the preservation and public display of artistic masterpieces, for instance, should also be encouraged from an ethical perspective. In this way, not only has the ethical subject broadened, as noted in the previous section, but the object of ethics has also expanded. In that respect, *eco-ethica* entails taking individual ethics to a deeper level.

A RESTRUCTURING OF VIRTUE ETHICS (ARETOLOGY)

New times call for many new virtues. In relation to the broadening of the ethical subject, we should foster the virtue of mutual respect so that the inclusion of groups and organizations as ethical subjects does not degenerate into nationalism or racialism. Establishing *tolerance* in a new sense is essential. Tolerance originally consisted of forgiving others for their mistakes. In the eighteenth century this broadened to acceptance of other people's religions. Taking this a step further to encompass acceptance of others' ideologies and values is, I believe, a prerequisite for coexistence. Here *philoxenia* comes into play as a new virtue. In isolation, however, this would merely mean reaching a low-level temporary compromise on denigrating each other, without any principled basis, and eventually we would end up at odds over our competing interests. Hence metaphysical speculations about values need to be taken to a deeper level in order to act as the basis for the possibility of a universal ethics grounded in humanity. The foundation for this lies in the desire to create morals, based on efforts to complement the intellectual legacy of the human race through a dialogue among different cultures. This is premised, however, on expressly learning the logic inherent in the language that is an intrinsic element of the cultural sphere to which one belongs. In that sense, comparative studies of manners and customs from a philosophical perspective are a topic for *eco-ethica* to address.

The characteristics of ethical systems are also said to derive initially from the kind of virtues formulated by the system. Since virtue ethics is an important issue, I intend to discuss this in detail on another occasion in the near future.

ISSUES RELATING TO HUMAN LIFE

In terms of virtues concerning the broadening of the ethical object, from the viewpoint of an ethics toward things there should be certain virtues that are expected not in relation to human existence but in relation to human life. Note that "things" does not refer here to material things. As the Japanese word for *person* (*jinbutsu* 人物, literally 'person-thing') shows, *things* is a profound and encompassing concept. In that sense, life is a thing.

Bioethics is an important concept in clinical medicine. This was originally a code of practice aimed at ensuring that doctors would use discretion in exercising their medical skills. The *eco-ethica* that I have in mind, however, is a system of fundamental ethics—one that can simultaneously act as the basis for a code of practice and way of thinking in the field of bioethics.

It is encouraging to see ethical awareness receiving renewed attention in various sectors of society today. Politicians are in agreement on the need for a political ethics, while people who have given thought to environmental matters argue that not only laws but also ethical awareness—i.e., environmental ethics—is vital, and various occupation-specific ethics have been proposed, such as *techno-ethica* (ethics relating to technology) and *arti-ethica* (ethics for the arts). These are along the lines of codes of practice that involve an ethical awareness. One reason for such discussions is the failure of conventional ethics to develop innovative ways of thinking that are capable of addressing such new issues and situations. Unlike the ethical codes in all sorts of occupational domains, however, *eco-ethica* possesses a scholarly system that can, as a fundamental meta-ethical reflection, also be extrapolated to those domains.

When we think about human life, one major issue that comes to mind along with brain death is organ transplants, which have become possible through medicine's collaboration with science and technology. Most *eco-ethica* researchers are advocates of organ transplants. Although I doubt that opposing such procedures will make any difference to this trend, I do not believe that, as matters stand at present, such procedures are a good thing. Survival should not come at the expense of depriving others of life, and to me liver transplants from a living donor seem to rob the donor of a little life, and waiting for an organ donor to die is tantamount to hoping someone will die soon, which is little different from willing someone's death. In my view, the desire for another's absence amounts to evil. Fundamentally, therefore, I believe that operations of this kind foster evil, so I question their ethicality. Yet this does not mean that I favour obstructing medical progress that is doing its utmost to fulfil people's natural desire for healing, or that I would abandon those in suffering. I believe that medicine and science and technology must move toward the development and practical use of artificial organs, no matter how difficult that might be at present. In my view this suggests one direction that at least has ethical grounds. A logical basis is an absolute necessity for a scholarly discipline.

LOGICAL ISSUES

In that sense this book incorporates logical considerations to an extent rare in works on ethics. The classical and contemporary syllogisms of action, a new taxonomy, a new form of abstraction—all these are mere steppingstones from which to pursue logic further, but they also represent important turning points in logic and constitute axes for constructing *eco-ethica*.

With these prefatory remarks by way of a simple introduction, let us now move on to the main discussion. I would greatly appreciate hearing from readers as to their views and suggestions.

I would like to express my heartfelt gratitude to the many people who helped me bring this book to fruition—Rudolph Berlinger, who has been a source of constant support; my old friends Luigi Pareyson, Paul Ricœur and Kōichi Tsujimura; Toyosaburō Taniguchi, sponsor of the International Symposium on Eco-ethica; the scholars from Japan and abroad with whom I have shared accommodation during this week-long symposium each year; and in particular the members of the standing committee, Professors Peter McCormick, Marco Olivetti, Megumi Sakabe, and Noriko Hashimoto.

Thanks too to Associate Professor Hashimoto for her tireless reading of the manuscript and her suggestions; to Naomi Wakai, who undertook the proofreading; to Yōichi Ikenaga, head of the Gakujutsu Bunko Publishing Department that kindly consented to include this book in Kodansha's Gakujutsu Bunko series; and to Mitsuko Nunomiya, who dedicated herself to the copyediting and various other tasks. Professors Juichi Katsura and Takezō Kaneko, as well as my friends Professor Keiichi Ōshima and Professor Wataru Kuroda, had long anticipated the appearance of this book. It is sad that they are no longer with us to witness its publication.

Tomonobu Imamichi
30 September 1990

Preface to English Edition

The publication of the English translation of my little book, *An Introduction to Eco-Ethica*, and its widespread introduction to scholars and readers around the world are a truly great honour and a great joy for me. I am sure this is also gratifying to my research group colleagues who have joined forces in supporting the development of this new field at the annual International Symposium on Eco-ethica that has been held for the past 26 years since 1981 (and which will continue to be held in the future). It is my hope that this book will reach a broad readership through the medium of English, a language that is widely understood throughout the world, because the world is in need of a new ethics. I hope that my ideas will be understood through this book, and even more so is it my wish that the meaning of the philosophical issues raised here will be conveyed to readers and that each individual reader will consider these issues and present his or her own solutions in a variety of different forms. In that sense, the fact that such an experienced academic as Dr. Judy Wakabayashi has translated this book so accurately is not only a matter of personal honour to me but also a boon to the academic world, and I would like to express my deep gratitude to her on both counts.

The Japanese original of this book was published in 1990, and already more than twenty editions have been issued. Well over a decade has passed since the first edition, so new issues have arisen during that time, and naturally these necessitate some revisions to the book, although the fundamentals remain unchanged. Taking the opportunity of the publication of the English edition and with the translator's cooperation, I have made several additions and revisions, paying particular attention to those parts. In the German translation that appeared in 2007, corrections were made to my careless errors in the names of the scholars who have worked with me.

The first foreign translation of this book was a Korean version by Professor Myong-hwan Jung that was published over a decade ago. Looking back on that now, I feel that the web of eco-ethica research might gradually spread in East Asia, and perhaps this English version will accelerate that trend. Let me add that our Centre International pour Étude Comparée de Philosophie et d'Esthètique has already published twenty-four volumes of the proceedings of the annual International Symposium on Eco-ethica, the *Revue Internationale de Philosophie Moderne*.

The English translation of my little book is the outcome of the good offices of Professor Seizō Sekine of the Ethics Department at the University of Tokyo and the translation support offered by the department's Watsuji and Matsumoto Fund. Let me conclude by expressing my heartfelt appreciation for the friendship of Professor Sekine, who has a distinguished reputation both in Japan and abroad, my indebtedness to Professor Tetsurō Watsuji, my mentor ever since my student days, and my gratitude for Dr. Wakabayashi's excellent translation.

Tomonobu Imamichi
July 2007

Chapter One

Preliminary Thoughts on the Essence of *Eco-ethica*

The focus of this chapter is the nebulous topic of just what constitutes *eco-ethica*. It is a new ethics offering an entirely fresh perspective, a groundbreaking ethical system that addresses ethical issues facing society today, such as bioethics and medical ethics, political ethics, environment ethics, and *techno-ethica*. This is a vital field, so I would like to start out by presenting my current thinking on these issues.

Eco-ethica refers to an ethics that encompasses our human habitat. It is one branch of an emerging philosophy aimed at rethinking how we live, including the various new issues facing the human race today, when society consists of a technology-mediated environment. My goal here is to discuss the fundamental issues, yet in a logical order and as accessibly as possible.

Let me start by delving into etymological matters in some detail. The *eco* in *eco-ethica* is the same as that in *ecology*. Ecology is usually called *biology*, which is the term mainly used in conjunction with the disciplines of geography, zoology and botany. *Ecology* originated in the word *ecologie* that the German scholar Ernst Häckel coined in the latter part of the nineteenth century out of biological or biogeographical necessity. For instance, when forests are logged, the animals are forced to seek a new habitat, so it is not enough to simply study individual animals in zoos. The word *ecology* was coined out of a desire to study animals in their natural habitat.

Eco was originally a Latin transliteration of the Greek οἶχος. In its narrow sense this means 'house', but more broadly it signifies habitat or surroundings, which is the usage adopted here. *Eco-ethica*, however, is a Latin term of my own invention. Here *eco* signifies human beings' habitat, so it includes the world of technology that will be discussed later. Rather than adopting the nation as the supreme ethical unit, however, *eco-ethica* is open to all people

1

across national boundaries—i.e., it is an ethics for a borderless society. Since the *eco* in *eco-ethica* signifies habitat in the broad sense, *eco-ethica* represents an ethics not for the family or the nation, but for our contemporary world with its scientific and technological environment. *Eco-ethica* is a moral science that addresses issues concerning our entire human habitat.

This calls for a new discipline. State theory and political science have existed to date, but nowadays cities constitute a habitat in a highly technological society, so there is a need for a real science of cities—a philosophy of the city, or *urbanica*. It is vital to consider cities from a philosophical perspective that differs from the approaches adopted in urban sociology. Nor does metaphysics suffice. In the past our environment consisted of a natural environment (*physis*, i.e., nature) that was the object of study in the discipline of *physica* (physics). The discipline of *metaphysica* (metaphysics) subsequently emerged to transcend this. Today, when *technica* (technology) is such an integral part of our environment, I would suggest the need for a *metatechnica* (metatechnics).

At the time I proposed these three fields, I happened to be in charge of the research projects subcommittee of the Fédération Internationale des Sociétés de Philosophie (International Federation of Philosophical Societies), so my proposal was taken up at one of our committee meetings as an important issue that needed to be addressed. Fortunately, Professor Raymond Klibansky and Professor Leo Gabriel, who were both senior and leading members, were kind enough to turn their attention to this, as did Paul Ricœur and Jean Parain-Vial. My ideas met with particular acceptance among the younger generation of scholars. In response to a suggestion that *eco-ethica*, the most urgent of these three issues, be made a focus of international study, an international research organization was established in 1974, and as the originator of this idea, I became the chairperson.

After several years of preparation and with the support of the Taniguchi Foundation, twenty-three international congresses on *eco-ethica* have been held in Japan, with the first one taking place in 1981. The proceedings (*Revue Internationale de Philosophie Moderne*) have been published by the Centre International pour Étude Comparée de Philosophie et d'Esthètique in Tokyo, with the papers being written in various European languages. Each issue carries a dozen or so papers on *eco-ethica* by Japanese and non-Japanese scholars, and over a hundred papers have been published so far. The pages of the *Revue* are replete with contributions by leading European scholars, outstanding Japanese scholars, and prominent scholars from other parts of Asia. The contributors also include up-and-coming scholars from Japan and around the globe. It is unusual anywhere in the world for so many papers on a single philosophical theme to be published in every issue of a journal for over two decades, and the *Revue* has won a growing international reputation in academic circles. In addition to scholars specializing in this field, I would urge journalists working in culture-related areas to take a look at the journal. Criticisms and suggestions from a broad spectrum of readers are welcome.

This research organization is a low-key group, and although it has received support from a few benefactors, it has not attracted much public attention. Fortunately, however, I have been given the opportunity to present my lectures on *eco-ethica* in this book, and I am delighted to have the chance to receive feedback from a wide spectrum of readers.

WHY ETHICS NOW?

I would like to move on to the substance of *eco-ethica*, but first there is one issue that needs to be addressed. This is the question of just why it is necessary to think about ethics at this point in time. As is appropriate with philosophy, we will start with a fundamental question—i.e., where are we now? To ascertain this in concrete terms, let us divide the question into two aspects: (1) What kind of society is our civilization? (2) What kind of society is our culture? I will restrict the scope of the first topic to material objects. As far as these are concerned, our civilization is an institution where the general public has access to convenient mechanical gizmos that surpass those available to royalty and titled nobility in the old days. It is a technological space that consists of a technology-mediated environment supported by the dual structure of the *modern nation* on the one hand and *globalization* as a negation of this on the other hand. In relation to the second aspect, our culture is generally the site of the historical process of human liberation. From the mid-nineteenth century onwards this has been a human rights space where we have witnessed the establishment of what can be summed up as fundamental human rights—e.g., the emancipation of slaves and serfs, equal rights for men and women, the abolition of discrimination against outcasts, the enactment of laws for the welfare of people with physical disabilities, and the abolition of racial discrimination.

Although the world in which we dwell should, under the banner of science and technology and human rights, be a happy one, the reality is different. We are exposed to the threat of seven 'untimely deaths'—i.e., starvation, death from accidents, death in war, death from pollution, death through terrorism, suicide, and murder. These existed in the past, but today atrocious terminations of human life, which should be protected through technology and human rights, are far more common than in any previous century. Admittedly, the rapid increase in total world population inflates the figures for deaths in all categories, but is it acceptable to use this as an excuse and merely fold our arms? Even if we take just the statistics for deaths in combat, can we simply stand by, knowing that in the seventeenth century the figure stood at 7 million, in the nineteenth century it had risen to 19.4 million, and in the mid-1980s it reached 107.8 million (*World Military and Social Expenditures*, 1987)? Naturally, such figures are not entirely accurate. Nevertheless, historians agree that the number of people killed in wars in the twentieth century alone far exceeded the number since the start of recorded history up until the end of the nineteenth century. Even though population growth is the main factor, we need to investigate the other causes behind this sudden increase in untimely deaths. We must not turn the twenty-first century into a century of massacres like the twentieth century.

I have formulated a contrary opposition between death and virtue. This is an idea that I have tested in various papers over many years to date, but since I want to move on, here I will simply summarize my findings.

THE CONTRARY OPPOSITION BETWEEN DEATH AND VIRTUE

In the past, cardinal virtues and technological virtues were variously discussed as key themes in ethics, but today, I would suggest, these have generally been forgotten. The four classic cardinal virtues ever since Aristotle are justice (*dikaiosynē*), practical wisdom (*phronēsis*), courage (*andreia*) and moderation (*sōphrosynē*) (the more widely known Latin terms for these virtues are *justitia*, *prudentia*, *fortitude* and *temperantia*), while the three traditional theological virtues of Christianity are faith (*fides*), hope (*spes, esperantia*) and love (*caritas, amor*). The basic definition of justice is the equitable distribution of things, and if only people had a sufficient awareness of this, then in today's world, where it is possible to increase production and a powerful transport system is available, the number of people dying from starvation would surely have fallen drastically. Practical wisdom means neither excess nor deficiency, and if working conditions were more balanced, then the number of accidents caused, for instance, by drivers nodding off at the wheel would also decrease. Courage entails unhesitatingly speaking out on what one believes is right, and if people had possessed such mettle, then perhaps World War II might have been avoided in the mid-twentieth century. We would have been wholeheartedly opposed to people of any nationality at all becoming soldiers and dying. If people had had the courage to speak out without hesitation, there would have been fewer deaths in the war. Although looking back on history through the lens of a particular assumption is not always appropriate, in the 1940s not a single person of my acquaintance agreed with the policies of the military government, yet sound arguments were overshadowed by the public silence, and the number of people killed in the war skyrocketed. Reading *Harukanaru sankai ni* (Far-off mountains and seas; Iwanami Bunko), an anthology of writings by students who fell in the war, gives real insights into the wartime anguish of young Japanese intellectuals. Moderation is the suppression of human desires. Death from environmental pollution is the result of companies' desire for economic profits, which is bolstered by consumers' demands for convenience. If we possessed the virtue of moderation, the number of people dying from pollution would decline.

Terrorism is a distortion of the virtue of faith. Here *belief* is absent. No religions or ideologies condone the killing of innocent others. Holding the killing of others as a tenet constitutes not belief, but unbelief and fixation. Hope is the desire for salvation, and life is the path toward that end, so hope should overcome any inclination toward suicide. Finally, love of course consists of regarding others as the object of neighbourly love and valuing them as one values oneself, so in such a situation killing others is unimaginable, which means that by rights murder should be inconceivable.

I would suggest that the current frequency of these seven types of untimely death is the result of having forgotten the seven above-mentioned virtues in this world in which we reside today. The forgetting of virtue is tantamount to the absence of virtue. Virtues lie at the core of ethics. The world in which we dwell has become a place devoid of ethics. People are acting on the basis of laws and customs, without ethics. This is why we need to think about reinstating ethics.

I will now move on to a consideration of this topic. Although reviving classic ethics is necessary in order to breathe new life into ethics, I would question, however, whether this alone is sufficient. The revolutionary creation of a new ethics is also essential.

THE UNPRECEDENTED ETHICAL ISSUES RAISED BY NEW TECHNOLOGY

The need for a new moral science can be conceptualized from various perspectives, but let's begin with some close-to-home issues in *eco-ethica*. One is the relationship between moral science and categorical imperatives of religion—i.e., categorical statements based on a religious viewpoint. Originally these statements and moral science had always followed the same trajectory, but nowadays there is a rift between the two.

Let me cite an obvious example. When God created humankind, as outlined in Genesis in the Old Testament, one of his first exhortations was to "Be fruitful and increase in number and fill the earth". At the dawn of the human race a quantitative expansion of the species was one of the most desirable goals. This line of thought was valued for generations to come, and it merged with the idea of a 'wealthy nation and a strong army'. At any rate, it was long deemed desirable for families to have as many children as possible and for nations to train them into a skilled populace. Nowadays, improvements in our living environment have led to a rapid decline in infant mortality and deaths from epidemics, but this has also resulted in concern over the population explosion.

We live in a time when economic conditions and civilization are very advanced, yet an unprecedented number of people have starved to death or are facing death from starvation. The reality is that our world is over-populated, outstripping the human race's capacity to produce food and manage the food supply. So advanced countries that are apprehensive about their own future and concerned over the future of humankind have no choice but to adopt birth-control measures out of social or national policy considerations or, to take matters further, from the viewpoint of the entire human race.

Hence contraception for married couples is now taken for granted. Beyond that or in particular situations, the legality of abortions has also become a topic of discussion. Even if there are moves to ban abortion on the grounds that it is tantamount to murder and adversely affects the mother's physical and mental wellbeing, the important point here is that having and raising many children together is not necessarily what constitutes the bond between a married couple. The idea that sexual intercourse that is regarded as legitimate only for married couples leads to progeny—i.e., the idea of old religions that sexual pleasure exists as a sort of advance compensation for the travail and efforts involved in giving birth to and raising children—generally meets with a prima facie rebuttal. So intercourse without contraception is logically validated as a pleasure not based on the premise of having children. This then calls into question the grounds for moral views that would restrict sexual intercourse to married couples.

Following this line of thought also leads to the conclusion that sex using contraceptives is ethically acceptable as an expression of love—and not just between married couples. This would in turn lead to a revolutionary sexual ethics at odds with the moral traditions of Christianity, which advocates a civil society centred on the family, and also at odds with those of Confucianism. Moreover, it would give rise to doubts about the primacy of the family. The pros and cons of these ideas need to be put forward.

In highly technological societies work is carried out with the aid of machines, so physical strength is no longer always required. As all kinds of occupations become mechanized, the idea of equal rights for men and women arises across the fabric of society, not so much in terms of equal rights as human beings, but as the concept of equal labour power. This triggers a clash between ethical concepts and the religious ideas of Confucianism and Christianity, whereby men and women should engage in different kinds of work. Unless ethics is established in such situations, the foundations of education will also be undermined.

In the past ethics was backed by religion on truly crucial fundamental issues, but in today's highly technological society there is a tendency for religions as a whole to lose their social clout, and it has become common for the behaviour of people in general to be simply regulated by machines. If things continue like this, ethics runs the risk of turning into mere platitudes with no substance. The result would be a society devoid of ethical principles, an assemblage of individuals who had lost their way. There is a need to formulate an ethics that, unlike conventional *ethica*, is fully cognizant of the ecological changes facing humankind, which is why I came up with the term *eco-ethica*.

An awareness of oneself as a minority always leads to an elite consciousness that sets oneself, charged with some weighty mission, apart from the general populace. In a time when the economy is doing well, people's livelihoods are stable, the number of students wishing to go on to higher studies is on the rise and new universities are constructed and forty to fifty percent of young people are able to proceed to tertiary studies, university students can no longer be regarded as an elite. In such situations intellectuals generally lack a sense of responsibility as the elite, and a surfeit of such intellectuals is common in highly technological societies. This surfeit is, I believe, a pathological phenomenon in highly technological societies. There's something wrong when what has been learnt at facilities provided by society is simply directed toward satisfying an individual's desires, with little interest in giving back to society.

Records show that in the Meiji period (1868–1912) Japan was full of young people with a sense of themselves as an elite. From our contemporary vantage point this does smack somewhat of the conceit of people from the countryside, but it could also be seen as an energy force whereby in ethical terms the desire to get on in the world functioned to suppress the self and worked to the benefit of the nation and society.

I wish that increased national power had not only afforded us the leeway to recognize that culture is a supranational matter, but had also brought home the concept of a supranational society—the human race. As long as people fail to realize the concreteness of culture, however, culture will never be more than a matter of self-development. So when they hear the word 'culture', people immediately think only of personal self-development (*Bildung*). This trend has been exacerbated in our technological society, where culture becomes a mere pastime, an ancillary pursuit that adds only to the individual's refinement and lacks any innate role in society itself, which is the locus of the individual's existence.

People think that studying Homer and Racine or the *Kojiki* (Records of Ancient Matters, 680 C.E.) or the ancient Japanese poetry anthology known as the *Manyōshū* is not a prerequisite for citizens in our technological society. They argue that studying such classics ultimately contributes to the accomplishments of that individual alone, and culture is not essential to advanced technology itself. They are not rejecting culture, but simply setting it apart. People believe that culture is being valued if specialists attach importance to certain parts of culture as an object of study and individuals pursue certain aspects of culture out of personal interest.

It is true that culture has not been rejected in highly technological societies, but nor is it regarded as indispensable. Its treatment in technological societies, where it is not deemed essential but instead set apart and respected, can even be regarded as a matter of policy on the part of these societies, such that it is impossible to have people adopt a decisive attitude toward culture. People feel that since it is being valued, it's fine for culture to become a means of leisure (*schole*) as the pastime component of society that has split off at that point. So people compartmentalize culture and isolate each segment within technological society.

By rights, however, culture is a single entity, and although it can indeed take the form of pursuits that are discrete individual cultural phenomena or take the form of individual specialized disciplines and arts, it should be an organic whole. As such, it must incorporate ethics and morals. When technological society does not view culture as essential, it fails to regard the organic whole that is culture as a vital component of society, which in turn means that ethics might not be seen as indispensable.

The fact that technological societies encourage individuals to value particular sectors of culture means that ethics is valued as one cultural sector amongst many and as the pursuit or concern of individuals. We could argue that in technological societies ethics is not regarded as intrinsically indispensable. As long as machines dictate all behaviour and people act accordingly, everything should be fine. All that is needed is to act in accordance with coded instructions.

If we assume that acts performed at the behest of machines should be ethical, then machines in technological societies must at least incorporate ethical principles. Yet what machines enable is improved efficiency and greater convenience. This represents a quantitative increase in the production of identical goods, as well as labour-saving in the production process, but ultimately it is just a saving of time. If we assume that temporality should be regarded as a venue where human awareness arises, then the world of machine technology has a structure that compresses temporality and hence awareness and, in turn, ethical thinking as the core of human awareness.

In this way our world today is moving toward abandoning all consideration of ethical issues. Teaching along the lines of ethics is already far from adequate in Japanese elementary and junior high schools, and even when subjects such as the history of ethical thought used to be taught at senior high schools under the rubric of 'ethics and society', ethics itself came in for little attention. The subject of ethics and society has also recently disappeared from the high school curriculum, being renamed civics, so that ethics is now absent from the teaching of matters to which individuals and the human race need to give thought. Of course, as the government body responsible for overseeing education in Japan, the Ministry of Education has its reasons for this and would no doubt argue that it is emphasizing moral education and thoroughly inculcating this at schools. Yet many teachers mistake morals for discipline, and if we ignore ethics, which considers morals from an ethical perspective, we are no longer thinking about morals.

In Europe too, ethics education—a function that used to be filled by religion at the secondary school level—is now becoming an elective course. The more technological a society becomes, the more neglected is ethics. Universities have classes on ethics and stress its importance, but such classes mainly consist of the history of ethical theories. Although important as an academic discipline, this relegates ethics to the status of merely one aspect of culture, along with classes in art history, French literature and aesthetics. It is not something that is studied as the universal foundation of our lives. It might be no exaggeration then to argue—as does, for instance, the *meta-ethica* scholar Richard Mervyn Hare—that even in the discipline of ethics itself in such situations ethics fails to go beyond the study of *meta-ethica* as a logical analysis of ethical propositions, or beyond the study of the history of ethical theories.

A scholar called Griebendorf has suggested that today only second-order ethics continues to flourish. First-order ethics considers fundamental questions such as what is good, how we should act, what is prohibited, and what is allowed. By contrast, *meta-ethica* constitutes an ethical analysis of moral propositions based on such postulates put forward by others. Specifically, meta-ethics is the analysis of moral predicates such as 'good' and 'proper' and of moral expressions such as anger at betrayal. This alone does not constitute ethics as a discipline. As the philosopher Tetsurō Watsuji once said, we must value the accomplishments achieved by ethics as a factual discipline, but such an approach ultimately boils down to questions of the history of ethical theories, such as what kind of ethical thought existed in a particular place at a particular time. Hence this is a historical description of moral thinking.

Such matters are of course important for a discipline, but with that approach relatively little heed is paid to the fundamental concept of what kind of issues are ethically established as acts to be encouraged. In my view this approach epitomizes the treatment, as well as the self-regulation, of ethics in highly technological societies. I believe that a preliminary classification of the propositions with which ethics should engage leads to the following four categories:

1. the study of particular moral propositions or moral ideas as held by a particular society or scholar.
2. propositions that express a logically substantiated attitude toward such propositions and ideas. Ultimately, this boils down to agreement with or criticism of their moral substance.
3. analysis of the meaning of words and expressions used in the first two categories.
4. descriptive and historical corrections of the issues in the above categories—i.e., the history of ethical theories.

By no means am I disparaging these approaches. In reality, such matters constitute the state of general ethics, and they are necessary as basic research. Nevertheless, in the latter part of the twentieth century we have come to feel that this alone is inadequate and that we must formulate ethical propositions of substance. Rather than simply studying what propositions once existed in a certain period, we should put forward our own new propositions. This is likewise the aim of *eco-ethica*. So *eco-ethica* as considered here essentially falls into none of the four categories above. It constitutes a fifth category, a revolutionary experiment in ethics.

Since this involves the formulation of ethical propositions that have a certain substance, it is a normative ethics, which might seem to belong to the first category. What is envisaged here, however, is an entire system, which includes the presentation of moral propositions such as the establishment of new virtues. This means that we must consider the connection with technology (i.e., the technology-mediated environment), which is the essence of modern society, so in that sense we need to address the *metatechnica* that takes the place of *metaphysica*. And since the city as a life form is a venue that specifically calls for such an ethics, within *metatechnica* we need to consider *urbanica* (i.e., the philosophy of the city), rather than the *politica* (political science) of the past. In that sense, I think this new ethics must take on a form akin to the *Weltwissenschaft* (world science) proposed by Rudolph Berlinger.

Based on two different critiques of moral propositions, *eco-ethica* arrives, therefore, at the establishment of innovative moral propositions, yet it seems to me that a new fifth domain—i.e., a consideration of the moral issues facing the human race as a result of changes in our habitat—might occupy a major position between these. *Eco-ethica* aims at an overall rethinking of conventional ethics, taking this aspect on board.

Hence I believe we need to consider the changes in our ontological structure and the multipolarity of relationships today. As Watsuji has pointed out, the fact that ethics is the study of betweenness (*aidagara*—i.e., the relationality of man) is extremely important. Also discernible here is the trend whereby Gabriel Marcel transformed *intersubjectivité*—i.e., Edmund Husserl's epistemological *Intersubjectivität*—existentially and attempted to lay ethics as the foundation for the study of existentialist *intersubjectivité*. In that sense ethics was regarded as the study of relationality among people.

We should think carefully about whether to accept this claim. Ethics is undoubtedly the study of relationships. The idea ever since Aristotle that fundamentally regards humans (*anthropos*) as social animals and that views people as coexisting beings has been around since olden times. Yet surely there are aspects of relationships that differ between when our environment consisted of nature and when technology has become part of our environment? In my opinion, we need to focus on this fact first, because the environment affects relationships.

The relationships that human beings have in a natural environment range from those that are essential for just about any life form—such as the role-sharing that derives from communal living (e.g., parent–child, siblings, husband and wife, master–servant) as well as enemy–ally—right through to various relationships found even in higher-order animals. All of these boil down to direct biological relationships among individual creatures or to functional sociological relations for group living. The emergence of relationships not found in the animal world or natural life is, I believe, an issue of our present times in which technology constitutes our environment.

First we need to consider the various relationships formed through reason, an attribute found only in human beings. Top of the list here is the fact that—through linguistic relationships, which are mediated by language and differ in nature from semiotic behavioral responses—human beings can not only relate to concepts but are also able to construct all kinds of autonomous worlds and form relationships with these. Naturally, we need to take this issue into account when thinking about human beings. Since these relationships do not involve relationships among individual entities, they will not be discussed in this chapter, but they must be regarded as a new form of relationship.

What does need to be noted in terms of relationships among individual entities, however, is the fact that in the case of human beings indirect relationships have been formed through a medium. In other words, when the two technological activities of production and management come into being in a sophisticated form, relationships among individual entities are no longer limited to natural, accidental directness, but are characterized by technological, inevitable indirectness. Unlike situations where a natural relationship already exists among individual entities as life forms and the problem of allocation of materials arises subsequently, with these new relationships among individual entities technological materials exist from the outset in the form of an artificial physical structure, and non-physical relationships come into being as a result of this. In that sense, these relationships are very different from natural relationships among individual entities in the past. The resulting dimension of human behaviour is one of indirectness that differs from the directness among individual entities. Here production includes not just the production of goods, but also production whose object is effectiveness—in itself an invisible force. And what is managed is not just the material existence of goods, but also their *energeia* (actuality), which is itself invisible—i.e., their value in terms of non-physical effectiveness.

For a specific example, we need to consider not just the production of goods, but also, for instance, the production of atomic energy. In that sense this also produces invisible *dynamis* (potentiality)—i.e., potential force. Of course, management involves managing the material existence of goods, but it also requires managing *energeia* that are themselves invisible—i.e., the object's value in terms of non-physical effectiveness (e.g., the artistic value of paintings and sculptures).

As a result, production gives rise to invisible relationships with an unspecified number of people—an infinite increase in our neighbours. Moreover, the increased productive capacity not only enables the pursuit of profits, but more or less directly enables the pursuit of power as well, so eventually it can lead to large-scale damage and harm in unseen places, with no suffering on the part of those exercising this power. Ultimately, this means that the limits of conventional ethics, which consisted of an *ethica facie ad faciem* (face-to-face ethics), have become apparent and ethics has broadened to encompass actions at distances that are beyond our direct perception and that can be controlled remotely.

In concrete terms, this means we need to rethink the concept of neighbour in ethics. In the past, our neighbours consisted of people with whom we had blood ties or territorial connections, but sometimes we also regard as neighbours people who are geographically distant and who would never naturally be regarded in that light. This occurs through legal ties or through work ties or through technological ties where people are linked by technology.

Let me give an example. The telephone brings someone in Paris closer than people in my own neighbourhood in the Tokyo region, where you can barely be heard if you shout out, so this even enables threatening phone calls to someone in Paris in the middle of the night. This allows people to form relationships through a sense of proximity despite the lack of any physical proximity. Voices and images, for instance, can easily be switched, so sometimes actions must be decided solely on the basis of information, without any voices or images.

This naturally calls for an ethics that differs from that of the past. The sole cause lies, I believe, in our changed life circumstances. It also becomes apparent that such changes are triggering a reversal in the syllogism of action. As to be expected, this is as serious an issue as the overturning of the concept of what constitutes a neighbour. I will consider the reversal of the syllogism of action logically and in detail in Chapter 4, but for now let me explain it briefly.

Ever since Aristotle action has been conceived of in terms of the syllogism of action. The major premise here is that an end is formulated as a certain desire. Let's suppose that A is desired—for example, someone wants money. Then the means (i), (ii), (iii), (iv) and so on that will enable A are listed in the minor premises. Aristotle classified these minor premises into two types. If, for instance, one chooses (i) as the means, one's objective may be achieved "in the most expedient and noblest way" (*rhasta kai kallista*). So the upshot is that this means taking option (i). The minor premises constitute the site of selection—i.e., the choice of the means.

This logical form remains alive in our private life even today, but on the social and public scale a completely different logical structure has emerged. Here the means are massive and an axiomatic given. For instance, suppose that a certain government possesses huge capital (*l*). This leads to the possibilities A, B, C and D being listed as the minor premises. Various ideas are put forward as to how to use this huge capital—such as utilizing it for energy development, investing in education, building up the military forces, or becoming a welfare state. Selecting the purpose is a fundamental issue in determining behaviour in the field of ethics.

Ultimately, the changes in our habitat, where technology and various means have become so powerful, have made us aware of the reversal in the syllogism of action for the first time, because such matters are nowhere to be found in existing books on ethics. Today the means are not something we choose. Instead, they exist as an axiomatic given, and what must be selected is the end purpose. With traditional ethics, the major premise usually involved decision-making by individuals—if I desire A, I choose (i) out of the means (i), (ii) and (iii) that will enable A. However, when we possess massive forces—capital and energy—and are wondering what end to put them to, it is the group, not the individual, that selects this goal, so the logical structure of committees inevitably becomes necessary within ethics as well. Just as individuals are responsible agents, so too should committees (groups) take responsibility, and it is not enough to simply subject them to legal regulation. This must be regarded as an ethical issue.

What I am saying is that there must be changes in the existential structure of relationships, as well as a new concept of neighbours as a consequence of this. Because of the structural reversal of the syllogism of action, we need to consider an ethics for committees—i.e., the question of responsibility must be considered as group ethics distinct from traditional ethics. Of course, there are many other issues involved, but these are starting points as one possible awareness for *eco-ethica*.

The difference between *eco-ethica* and what is known as environmental ethics is that new issues are emerging that require people to make autonomous decisions about their own actions, based not on the question of what to do about the environment (although of course it does include that) but on changes in our habitat occurring as a result of changes in our environment. In the following chapters, then, I would like to spell out the basic issues in *eco-ethica* step by step, focusing on the different types of problem.

Chapter Two

Reinstating Ethics

OUR RESPONSIBILITY TOWARD NATURE AND THINGS

Today, when our environment has become stratified into the domains of technology and culture, our life circumstances are obviously different from when our environment consisted solely of nature. This inevitably raises the question of whether ethics, as behavioral norms for living in this environment, might also undergo a change.

Tetsurō Watsuji, who taught ethics at the University of Tokyo and was one of my professors, wrote a voluminous three-volume work entitled *Rinrigaku*.[1] His small book called *Ningen no gaku toshite no rinrigaku* (Ethics as the study of human beings) was a prolegomena that signaled the basic argument adopted in *Rinrigaku*. Although this introductory work is along the lines of a textbook, it is a classic that is never out of print. In this work Watsuji analyzes the character *rin* 倫 from *rinrigaku* 倫理学 (ethics) and declares that since this refers to the people in one's circle, ethics is the study of *aidagara* (betweenness) among people. Ethics must indeed encompass this relationality aspect, and there is a history that has evolved along those lines. So it is not that I disagree with this idea, but what I want to raise here is instead the ethical question of the kind of attitude that human beings should now adopt toward nature. In other words, ethics must be broadened to include not just *ethica ad hominem* (interpersonal ethics), but also *ethica ad rem* (ethics toward things). Pollution problems, for instance, are relevant here. In the long run this does concern people, since it happens to them, but it includes an attitude of coexistence with nature. To put it another way, a sense of responsibility toward nature—or, more properly, responsibility for nature—is also becoming an essential ethical or moral awareness.

To give a quick example, if someone leaves empty cans that rust easily lying around on the ground instead of throwing them into a trash can, the rust will gradually seep into the earth, possibly killing off trees. When I see abandoned cars or refrigerators dumped in fields I am horrified to think that eventually the groundwater there will no longer be drinkable. If a plastic container is thrown away at the beach, it will not biograde, but will pollute the bay. So this is something we should all be concerned about. Unlike in the past, when it was merely a matter of the importance of a sense of public morality, people need to have an active sense of responsibility toward nature. In other words, I believe there is a need for an ethics or sense of morality in relation to nature.

On a larger scale, this leads to behavioral controls at the global level, such as the question of what measures to adopt in response to global warming or in order to protect life forms from excessive ultraviolet rays as a result of the destruction of the ozone layer by chlorofluorocarbons and other pollutants. All of these factors also act as a check on technological convenience and effectiveness and are suggestive as to the direction of scientific and technological research.

In terms of our cultural heritage, we have a duty to pass on to the next generation those works in which the brilliant minds of each period have in their own way enhanced human potential to the fullest, as well as a duty to enable the next generation to enjoy the same wondrous emotions these works have aroused in us. Note that it was after Europe became a civil society that the idea of museums or art galleries became widespread—i.e., after the eighteenth century. Up until then royalty and the aristocracy enjoyed the arts solely based on their own tastes and for private pleasure. In the twentieth century, however, the general public—not only in Europe and the United States, but everywhere—have come to believe that there are valuable works that should be preserved by the state or the human race. This calls not only for a sharing of the economic burden, so that our cultural heritage is jointly funded from taxes and entrance or tour fees, but also for ongoing mutual efforts to preserve and maintain these artifacts, and to make them accessible to the public, in the belief that on moral grounds too this cultural heritage should be made as widely available as possible. This too becomes an issue facing human beings synchronically and diachronically, but achieving this is impossible without a morality toward things. In other words, we have an ethical responsibility toward our cultural heritage, especially works of art.

Ethics, then, is not merely an issue of interpersonal relationships. We also need a sense of ethics toward nature and things in the broad sense of the term. So these matters also become topics for the new ethics of *eco-ethica*. In sum, then, we could say that *eco-ethica* expands the scope of ethics to include not just people, but also things.

CHANGES AFFECTING THE HUMAN HABITAT

We often hear the term 'human ecological change'. We need to realize that living conditions in our highly mechanical and technological environment—what I call the technology-mediated environment—or in an environment consisting of cultural assets are becoming different from when our environment consisted solely of nature. This means that the rules for living in such environments also differ, perhaps also leading to a revolution in behavioral principles. Let me spell out specifically the nature of these ecological changes in our lives.

The University of Tokyo's northern research institute is located in the Hokkaido town of Tokoro (I believe the name is of Ainu origins). This institute is a branch of the Department of Archaeology, and an associate professor and assistant are always there undertaking research. The ruins of pit dwellings can be found in this region. They belonged to people who lived there at quite an early stage, around the second or third century. Pit dwellings involve digging a hole and creating a room below ground, so there is no need to erect walls. The walls somehow come into being by positioning a pillar in the centre and covering the dwelling with a thatched roof—i.e., by digging down.

All of these pit dwellings—said to number two or three thousand in total—are located on low hills, but only about a hundred of these are being studied today. The hills receive good sunlight from the south, and to the north there are woods, which act as a natural wind barrier. Nearby is a river known as the Tokoro River, but since the houses are located on a rise, the water needed for daily life could be obtained simply by digging downwards, and even if heavy rains in the rainy season cause the river to flood, the houses are never inundated. Settlements used to develop in places such as this. That is the first point I would like readers to bear in mind.

Even today I work at the Centre International pour Étude Comparée de Philosophie et d'Esthètique, and I often use the subway to get there. The advertisements on the train often catch my eye, particularly the real estate advertisements. An examination of these shows that they always feature the fact that the houses for sale receive good sunlight, are on level ground, and are equipped with electricity, gas, water and air conditioning. In ancient times, when nature was our sole environment, people were forced to live near rivers, and they had to find sites that were natural hills and received good natural sunlight. Today it's ideal if these three natural conditions are met, but as long as air conditioning and gas and water facilities are available, you can live without a river nearby, and in a house that faces north and does not receive good sunlight. So even with quite poor natural conditions, you *can live* there as long as a technological infrastructure is in place. In other words, we are clearly able to lead a comfortable life in a technological environment. Of course, we need sun and air, so it doesn't mean that nature has disappeared, but we are forced to acknowledge that we live in an environment that consists of technology. This change has happened over an extremely long period of time.

Let's now turn to more recent changes that occurred in the six decades or so since the 1930s. In 1930 I had just entered primary school. In those days cars were still not a common sight. Gradually, however, the trains on which people commuted to school or work became more packed, and the expression 'rush hour' came into vogue. In large cities such as Tokyo and Paris primary school children ended up using the subway or buses or trains to get to school, and even in smaller cities children of all ages began to use public transport. Transport came to occupy a position in everyday life and to be related to people's actions and behaviour.

From around that time there began to be talk of previously unheard-of morals—i.e., traffic morals. In the old days there was no risk of killing or injuring someone while commuting, but at railway stations in crowded cities and in our automobile society a lack of awareness of traffic morals could prove fatal to oneself or others. This led to the formulation of traffic rules—starting with obeying traffic signals—and traffic laws. Thinking about how to obey and apply these rules and laws also heightens our awareness of traffic morals.

One fundamental aspect of traffic morals involves being careful not to cause trouble for others, and a further aspect entails being considerate to and helping others. The most common aspect, however, involves responding reflexively to traffic signals and traffic signs. This reality naturally leads to the idea that morals are a non-autonomous submission to social control. People treat themselves as parts of a machine, and we come to regard morals as akin to regulations aimed at achieving the benefits of functional necessity.

And in reality, from around the time that, as a result of these traffic morals, people began to think they must unquestioningly obey traffic signals as an identical social signal, the identification ethics of totalitarianism began to oppress people on a global scale by way of fascism, Nazism and militarism as ideological directives. Identicalization—i.e., adopting identicality as a principle of action—is extremely important in terms of logic, but needs to be treated with great caution as far as ethics is concerned.

ETHICS FOR LIVING *WELL*

A mechanistic worldview that tried to reduce human beings to machines and explain them in those terms was once very widespread. That was in the

1950s and 1960s. Unlike the humans-as-machines concept prevalent in the eighteenth and nineteenth centuries, this truly tried to reduce human beings to machines. This was because various effective structures had been devised to enhance the functional benefits that had been so emphasized since the war and because attention also focused on cybernetics and similar sciences, with robots and other labour-saving machines outdoing the work of humans.

The 1970s saw the emergence of strong views to the effect that although machines surpass human abilities to produce goods and to work, human beings possess life, which is of supreme importance and is something lacking in machines, and we should value this. Life is indeed precious, and medicine has devised various ways to extend it. Yet we need to stop and think whether trying to survive by any means available and valuing only the fact of physical life actually constitutes living in a truly human manner. On rare occasions we might encounter something we feel compelled to carry through with even at the cost of our life. There is a tendency to think that we have only one life and nothing is more valuable, but this would mean that we would derive the greatest value from taking advantage of others by the most devious and contemptible means possible and from living a life of deceit.

Yet is *merely* living our true goal? Is life the value to be most treasured? Or is living *well* (i.e., Plato's *to eŭ zên*) our goal? In other words, is the goal not *just* living, but living for the sake of a *particular* value? In that case, it seems there would be levels—a hierarchy—in the spectrum of values, including life itself. On the other hand, surely this hierarchy of values would be a subjective matter? One person would not regret risking his neck in an adventure, while another might sacrifice his life for the sake of love, and yet another might risk her life to save a drowning child. The French have a saying that 'to love is to die a little' (*aimer, c'est mourir un peu*). Be that as it may, loving someone means that you no longer hold your own life as the supreme value. When the Japanese folk hero Yamato Takeru-no-mikoto met with disaster at the sea of Sagami, his wife Princess Ototachibana cast herself into the waters in an attempt to quell the tyranny of the god of the sea by offering a human sacrifice, in accordance with the beliefs of the time. In the extremes of love, people are willing to give up their life for a loved one.

Just imagine, for instance, that the person you love most—a friend, your child or parent, your wife or lover—is hospitalized for an operation. Although we usually regard our own life as invaluable, at times we would be willing to die in someone's stead to save them, if it were possible, though we realize that our wish is futile. That is why I believe that the Bible passage "Greater love has no one than this, that he lay down his life for his friends" likewise means that if people value their own life, giving it up represents the greatest love that can move a person's heart.

I'm not sure if it is because people place importance on their work or on personal advancement, but sometimes they work overtime to the point of exhaustion and then the next morning head off for work in a packed train, still suffering from a lack of sleep and not even having had any breakfast. By no stretch of the imagination does this provide an optimum lifestyle. Behind such actions, however, lies the reality that people are working even at the risk of their life, although it's unclear whether they genuinely love their work or are seeking personal advancement or simply money. I would suggest that in such situations the value of life has become a source of energy for accomplishing their work. In this case, is not life actually being conceived of as having some other purpose, as a source of energy for achieving this goal? In this way, life is sacrificed little by little for a higher value. Without an understanding of this, one would lose one's ideals.

It is a well-known fact that during World War II certain people instilled in others the idea that the life of an individual citizen lies in dying for the nation. Many members of the public went along with this idea. The lives of individuals were regarded as of no account, as lighter than a feather. This is wrong. The state is merely one historical form, an institution that enables us to live together. Nevertheless, this wartime idea that held life to be of such little account persisted for some time even after the end of the war, perhaps because life then was so tough, and there were even newspaper advertisements proclaiming 'Life for sale'. Perhaps in reaction to this, in Japan today, decades after the end of the war, there are calls to value the lives of individuals, and an increasing number of people believe that life itself is the supreme value. They hold, too, that one must also value one's own life. Nevertheless, we should not forget the obvious fact that one's life should be consecrated to a value one wishes to bring about.

It is only when we recognize that life exists not *merely* for living, but for living *well*, that we can also think about the purpose of human life—i.e., what we are living for—and consider a philosophical ethics that questions what the *well* in 'living well' means. In this way, it logically becomes apparent that those worthy of admiration are not people who get their own way by killing someone and pinning the crime on another to save their own skin—those who protect their life in this way are not to be admired—but those who sacrifice their life for the sake of human dignity (for instance, to protect freedom of thought). The reason that the phrase "Itagaki may perish, but liberty will survive"[2] carries such weight is that these words sprang not from this politician caving in and taking the attitude of 'Spare me! I'll speak of liberty no more', in an attempt to save his own life, but because these words demonstrated the burning purpose to which he was willing to sacrifice his life.

WHY IS ETHICS BEING FORGOTTEN?

The major changes mentioned earlier are taking place in our everyday lives as a result of unprecedented advances in engineering technology. Our lives often seem isolated within an inevitable plan, incubated like a pure culture in biology, so that life becomes emotionally sterile. The upshot is that we no longer think about the meaning of life. Even a moment's reflection on this would in a sense require silence in the world. And in this silence we would need to examine ourselves.

To this very day I remember that as a boy I used to hear the rustling crack of falling leaves as they hit the walls in my garden, even in Tokyo. This was a sound that made even a young boy think of the autumn of the world and human mortality. Tokyo has now become a metropolis where such sounds are no longer audible to the human ear. It is as if social conditions have robbed us of this silence today. Electrical media surround us with a cacophony of sounds and images, so we lose even the time to look inwards. In the midst of this hustle and bustle people no longer ponder the purpose of life, and eventually they come to think of life as the single most important entity. This leads to an egoism that rejects ethics.

In a technological civilization people also start to think that living *well* means being surrounded by noises and living more effectively than others; no longer does it mean living for values for which one would be willing to give one's life. Instead, we come to believe that all creatures exist to benefit our life. Hence in our technology-mediated environment, or perhaps in all advanced societies, ethics is becoming forgotten.

In Japan, for instance, ethics is no longer part of the senior high school curriculum, and even at universities it is no longer a compulsory course for all students, unlike in the past. In society there are guidelines on how to act—i.e., in addition to instructions on how to operate machinery in a way befitting someone living in a technology-mediated environment, there are also rules on how to work as a member of a corporate entity. Behavioral guidelines in that sense do exist, but ethics that considers what we as human beings should hold as ideals and how we should behave has disappeared—even though nobody believes this is a satisfactory situation. To put it another way, while everyone agrees on the importance of ethics, it has been rendered powerless. So we need to consider just why this is so.

Why is ethics forgotten in technological societies? I would suggest that it might be because ethics is no longer capable of wielding any actual ethical force. In other words, the changes that we have experienced in our ecology have transformed the ethical conditions in our lives, yet ethics continues to cling to the ideas of yore.

How will technology change the world, and what is the state of ethics today? The most understandable example would be bioethics. Advances in the life sciences and medicine mean that today a host of issues touch on ethics, be that in relation to sex or medical treatment, and several new issues have also emerged. Yet those in the field of ethics—i.e., philosophers—have failed to be proactive in presenting any substantiated statements on either the pros or cons of these matters, and even if such arguments are put forward, nobody pays the slightest attention to them.

Putting an end to sexually transmitted diseases would benefit the human race but would lead to sexual liberation unconstrained by fear of such diseases, and also to calls for unfettered sexual freedom. Throughout history there has always been a gap between the public discourse on sex and what people really think. Yet we must now think clearly about what constitutes our publicly professed principles today. Otherwise, as stated in Chapter 1, if there are no grounds at all for limits on sexual intercourse, we will not even be able to educate our young people. Surely we need to present the rationales both for allowing and rejecting premarital and extramarital sex? And how should we regard same-sex love in the form of genital sex and physical contact? Even those religious traditions that have the potential to link moral theology to ethics, such as Judaism and Christianity, have failed to elucidate these points of controversy in purely ethical terms. If we adopt the view that AIDS is a divine punishment just because it is common among homosexual men, this fear will disappear if treatments for AIDS are found, as they have been for syphilis. Rather than being swayed by such ancillary phenomena, therefore, we need to think ethically about the pros and cons of same-sex love involving genital sex.

The same goes for the pros and cons of sex changes or of choosing the sex of babies by altering chromosomes, as well as the question of how to set limits on DNA (genetic) manipulation. Is it acceptable to regard all these issues as matters of individual freedom or of authoritarian determination by certain groups and, as a result, to consider them as ethically neutral issues and exclude them from the ambit of ethics? In my view it is absolutely essential to regard as belonging to the province of ethics such questions as whether there is a distinction between matters that we must accept as fate, those that allow the free development of individuality, and things that need to be changed through human agency. And the necessary foundation for considering such issues lies in metaphysics. This means that we must conceive of a new ethics grounded in metaphysics.

Is the current state of affairs in medicine acceptable, where in the fields of medical ethics and bioethics matters are often discussed as a pretext (self-justification) for medical technology? Saving lives is indeed ideal. Yet we really need to consider whether this is humanly permissible if there is a risk that saving one person might end up depriving others of their organs or harming someone else's life. Rather than shortsightedly jumping to conclusions about the merits or otherwise of organ transplants, we need to weigh up the ethical implications, having given full consideration to the many acts entailed in such transplants.

Why is it that these matters are basically settled in ethics committees that include few or no philosophers working on such issues? The way things stand at present, there is no forum for people who are constantly thinking about such issues to express their views. All of this is because the potential offered by science and technology has taken the lead, enabling us to fulfill our desires. This results in the belief that 'might is right', and the public dislike any constraint on 'might' in the form of ethics. More problematic, however, is the fact that many philosophers are out of step with the times. When society is facing difficulties, philosophers must get down and dirty and struggle to show their contemporaries the way ahead. With issues such as those confronting us today, philosophy must turn into concrete ethics and play a leading role.

Here I have simply touched on several issues that need to be addressed. Yet this has, I believe, revealed the following four points:

1. why *eco-ethica* is necessary
2. a sample of topics that *eco-ethica* needs to address in future
3. all of these topics are familiar issues with which we are confronted in our quest to live better lives
4. both for the present and the future, the discipline of *eco-ethica* should establish guidelines for human behaviour in technological society or in societies no longer based on technology.

As readers will be aware, proverbs represent the seeds of ethics or a general moral consciousness. Moral consciousness underpins proverbs, and if developed it can contribute much to systematic ethics. Conversely, therefore, when a proverb no longer holds true, the moral consciousness that it had supported recedes and the ethical system based on that collapses.

Take, for instance, the Japanese saying "The three houses across the road and the houses on each side", which is a reference to one's immediate neighbours. This could be regarded as a kind of proverb, and it means that in an emergency "A good neighbour is better than a brother far off." In other words, this saying manifests a kind of moral consciousness aimed at improving day-to-day relationships, whereby people living in the immediate vicinity must help each other out as friends. If your regard your own house as at the centre of a group of neighbours who help each other, this saying refers to the three houses across the way and the houses on each side of you—i.e., six houses in total.

Given the general traffic situation in today's technological society, however, the houses on each side are still our neighbours, but the three houses across the road can no longer necessarily be regarded in that light. You can't just dash across to them, because of the heavy traffic travelling along the major thoroughfare separating them from your house. In the urban structure, dynamic traffic conditions are an additional factor on top of static geographic conditions, so it is only natural that the concept of one's neighbours should also undergo a transformation. The fact that the spatial order based on natural geography has been destroyed through the intervention of such dynamic traffic conditions is one characteristic of the technology-mediated environment. For instance, when I leave my research institute in Chiyoda Ward in Tokyo, I can reach the city of Nagoya by Shinkansen Bullet Train faster than I can reach the university's Hachijōji Seminar House in Greater Tokyo. In the old days when people travelled by foot, it was far quicker to get to Hachiōji from Edo (the old name for Tokyo) than it was to travel to Nagoya.

When such a functional spatial order emerges as distinct from the natural spatial order and we also take media such as the phone into account, we could conclude that a far-off friend with a phone is more of a neighbour than someone nearby whom it is difficult to call. It is a convenient, albeit disturbing, fact that dialling the emergency number—i.e., an impersonal network—is of more help in an emergency than a neighbour who is physically nearby.

I'm not arguing that there's anything wrong with this. We must acknowledge the considerable benefits of the telephone. Yet we should also realize that this has major ethical ramifications. In other words, help in medical emergencies or with handling intruders—acts for which in the past we relied on the effective love of our neighbours—is provided better and more promptly by impersonal organizations that are set up on a legal basis and that are technologically equipped. For instance, if I hear a noise next door or an actual scream for help, it would be better to call the emergency number than to check things out myself, given my lack of physical strength. Again, there is nothing wrong with this, and it is an effective approach. Nevertheless, we must acknowledge that as a result the crucial importance of humanity, which neighbourly love manifests, is lost and this love turns into a mundane phenomenon.

We need to consider what happens to love when the meaning of neighbourly love is somewhat diminished. Neighbourly love does not allow any freedom of choice. Even if it is someone you don't like, you must love your neighbour wholeheartedly, as you love yourself. Since this is a love for someone who became your neighbour through circumstances, here love exists as fate. As noted earlier, however, neighbourly love is not particularly necessary today, and instead it is more effective in all matters to make use of the legal and technological infrastructure. If you are in trouble, it's quicker to call the emergency number than to ask a neighbour for help. This convenient setup means that the only kind of love remaining is love as the product of freedom of choice. Hence love comes to be regarded not as an imperative, but as something that exists by inclination.

Love is a cornerstone of ethics. Be it Confucius' benevolence, Buddha's compassion, or Christ's love, this was not to be equated with emotions and physical desire—it was a moral imperative. I wonder how many people truly think about the fact that such love once existed. The idea of love as a moral imperative has, I would suggest, vanished from the everyday consciousness of at least those Japanese and European students with whom I am acquainted. In fact I myself have forgotten that love is an imperative and that there is a love that is obligatory even if it is difficult.

In such circumstances, the relationship between religion and ethics tends to be severed, going beyond the rift mentioned in Chapter 1, and religion's persuasive power to appeal to ethics becomes attenuated and its reliance on ethics declines. We could say that the general foundation of consciousness that governs our actions inclines toward the emotions, physical pleasure, economic advantage and technological effectiveness, while morality as a check on these is no longer at least a public institution.

Yet this is not the sole responsibility of those who live in technological societies. We philosophers have also failed to go beyond advocating the morals that were formulated in a time when our environment consisted only of nature.

In my view, traditional ethics consisted of a face-to-face ethics (*ethica ad faciem*) that regarded as its behavioral radius and paradigm of conduct those acts where the spheres of perception and action more or less matched. But when the technology-mediated environment becomes part of our environment, in a certain sense we must take the view that ethics consisting solely of face-to-face ethics has come to an end. Of course, face-to-face ethics will not fall by the wayside in everyday relationships, but certain elements have appeared within ethics in the broad sense of the term that transcend face-to-face ethics. There are two factors behind this.

One is the expansion of our sphere of perception in a way that our sphere of behaviour cannot match. For example, if I see that at one of the three houses mentioned above a child has fallen over and hurt himself, even if I want to run across the road and help I cannot do so because of the heavy traffic. Even if my only option is to shout out to someone in a house across the road that "The kid next door has hurt himself and is bleeding, so can you please help him?", my voice will be drowned out. In such situations you can't quickly recall the phone numbers of the houses across the road, and there's no guarantee that you'll immediately be able to put your hands on the scrap of paper where you'd jotted down these numbers. So you end up calling the emergency number. Even if the local police station that takes your call is undergoing renovations and is no longer at its usual location, there's no need to go out of your way to raise the alarm at a different police station. The local station's phone number has been transferred, so as long as you have a phone you can contact them wherever they might now be. So in this case the phone has extended your sphere of behaviour beyond your sphere of perception.

In other words, in the past our sphere of perception and our sphere of behaviour coincided, but in technological society sometimes our sphere of perception is broader, while at other times our sphere of behaviour is broader. This issue, which transcends face-to-face ethics, is of crucial importance. With the advanced communications of today, it is the phone that makes us aware of neighbourliness in the sense of being within hearing range. So if we feel inclined to play a prank and give someone a scare in the middle of the night, we can do so. Because of the fear of being seen, it's not easy to set out in the middle of the night and bang on a neighbour's door and threaten to kill them, but making such threats by phone is quite possible, so some people take that cowardly option. In other words, it has become easy to carry out such offenses without affecting one's sense of shame toward others and without anyone knowing in any case. The same goes for silent phone calls.

Now that faxes have become commonplace, anonymous documents produced on computers—where the writer can no longer be identified from the handwriting—will probably be sent off to unexpected places. The sphere of activity of our unknown neighbours will also expand, for better or for worse. This means that nowadays we are 'unknown neighbours' to an unspecified number of people. That's how things stand in the technological society.

TURNING INTO SKILLED ANIMALS

So as the twenty-first century draws nigh, ethics faces a difficult situation, with science and technology having both positive and negative effects on culture—a situation that calls for efforts to formulate new virtues. Let us take a look at this.

The history of the human race shows that morals and ethics have achieved gradual progress, as noted earlier. Whether or not human beings have become moral, the number of virtues—which represent a manifestation of our yearning for morality—is gradually increasing. Even when the name remains the same, the content of traditional virtues is changing. When the human race is today in the midst of such a revolutionary event as the advent of the technology-mediated environment, we must ask anew why we have failed to realize this and have failed to reconsider the question of morals.

Let me give a very down-to-earth example. When I look around my room I see quite a few technological appurtenances. There's a clock and a cassette player and cassettes, as well as a phone and air conditioner. What sort of language do I use in relation to such devices? When I buy a new CD player and ask how to use it, the shop assistant says "When you push this button you can record. This button is for rewinding." Most people would then, like me, reply "Oh, I get it." But what does 'getting it' mean? In reality, we haven't understood a thing. Is comprehension such an easy matter? Knowing what will happen if you depress a switch or what function will be activated simply means that you've learnt how to operate the device. It is only when we understand *how* voices are recorded when we push a particular button or *how* pressing a switch changes the TV channel that we have achieved true understanding.

We say "I get it" despite not having a clue. Claiming to have understood a mechanism when we've merely learnt how to operate it is, I would suggest, a betrayal of language. When I enter the realm of machines and stand in front of what's popularly referred to as a 'black box', I feel as if I've understood it simply by getting the hang of operating that big box, even though I have no inkling of its inner workings. There I am in front of it, but apart from knowing how to operate it I have absolutely no understanding of how the setup works. And nor does the sales assistant. Only those who produced the device have any idea. So the salesperson and I are just saying "I get it", but all we know is which buttons to push, and we don't actually have a clue.

It is simply that we know what will happen if we press a particular button when told to do so, without making any use of our intellect, the pride of the human race. This is exactly the same as how animals get into trouble if they don't wait to eat when told to do so and how they start eating once given the okay, even though they have no understanding of the words at all. Even without such understanding, they are able to respond. If you don't believe me, try changing your tone gradually and saying "Okay" to your dog before you say "Sit". Your dog will still sit. If you then say "Sit" instead of "Stay", the dog will usually wait just as if it had been told to do so. Some dogs will even start eating if the final command is "Sit". Most dogs have no understanding of the meaning; they are simply responding in the order in which the commands are given.

If we suppose that human beings are moving in a similar direction, then in a sense we are descending to the level of skilled animals in our new society in the technology-mediated environment. As long as we too pretend to understanding despite not having a clue, comprehension degenerates into a matter of being able to operate something. If we ignore understanding and regard the mastering of skills as success, one might argue, for instance, that there's little difference between this and treating our children as animals, and that somewhere along the way we ourselves have become animal handlers in a circus. In fact, we are forced to realize that at some point we have turned into animals.

A similar situation exists in the world of morals. The old school subject of ethics did indeed have various drawbacks, such as its nationalistic tendencies, but through exemplars of virtuous conduct Japanese schools once made students think intellectually about morals, via this Confucian concept of ethics. After Japan's defeat in World War II, however, this subject was abandoned with alacrity, with no any attempt to revamp it or make it more broadly applicable. As a result, young people operate on the principle that you can't go wrong if you simply do what you've been trained to do courtesy of ethics. Phenomenologically, we might at least have been able to claim that this somehow led to good outcomes, but with this situation there is no theoretical underpinning for our behaviour, which is like hanging by a hair, and it's anyone's guess how far things might collapse in a major crisis.

In actual fact, this is what has happened. General Nogi had studied ethics, so he treated his enemy General Stessel with great courtesy when they met after the Russo-Japanese War, but when General Percival surrendered the Allied Forces to General Yamashita in Singapore during World War II Yamashita ordered him to come unarmed, and he thumped the table and yelled at him. Yamashita did not even observe *bushidō*, the feudal code of samurai ethics. Hence I believe we must all maintain the theoretical courage to seek out new virtues and new moral principles in contemporary society, no matter how difficult that might seem.

Unlike animals, human beings create art. Since these objects should be available for the enjoyment of future generations, and also in order to demonstrate to future generations just what wonderful things human beings are capable of, we should make efforts to preserve art masterpieces in their current form for as long as possible. If that is not morality, what is it?

This must give us pause. As I've stated repeatedly, ethics has focused on interpersonal ethics up until now. But from here on we must realize that there are other objects to which ethics directly applies, such as nature, technology and culture, so that the scope of *eco-ethica* has broadened. For instance, for a small entrance fee you can legally enter an art museum filled with masterpieces from remote antiquity. This is something for which we should be highly grateful. Through the legally determined entrance fees and through public taxes, art museums are able to cover their administrative and maintenance costs and look after all sorts of masterpieces. In this way we are protecting our cultural heritage. But some people pay the entrance fee and then proceed to damage the works on display. At St. Peter's Basilica, where there is no entrance fee, someone actually damaged the Pietà, Michelangelo's masterpiece. Even committing an outrage against a cultural asset simply results in a legal slap on the wrist for property damage or for violating the Law for the Protection of Cultural Properties.

How would morality impugn such an act? In terms of morals, there is still no label for this as an unethical act. According to the prohibition against damaging other people's property, there would be no difference between damaging this desk and daubing ink on a painting by Leonardo da Vinci. What more can I say?

ECO-ETHICA IN OUR DAY-TO-DAY LIVES

From this perspective, we realize that there are many issues of *eco-ethica* right on our doorstep. And unless scholars speak out on issues close to us, their ideas will not become part of society. So if there is any meaning at all in what I have so roughly sketched out here, it is that ethics and morals arise and dwell in situations close to hand, and this is precisely why if ethics disappears, human beings will break down starting from these everyday situations and they will no longer truly be human, instead turning into skilled animals in the technology-mediated environment. Merely responding to their environment is how animals live. Human beings, by contrast, have altered their environment. Rather than simply huddling up because it's cold, you try to make something to keep you warm. If you speak softly, you don't just run up to people—you make a microphone so that lots of people can hear you. Rather than submitting to our environment, we have transformed it through technology, seeking to transcend our natural environment.

If we respond passively to the technology-mediated environment that has emerged today, we will be going against our track record of trying to transcend our environment, and we will lose what makes us human. If that happens, morals will naturally fall by the wayside. And I believe that a decay in morals leads to spiritual decay.

In that sense, we need to formulate a new ethics and strive to protect human decency. This is the task of *eco-ethica*. In the process, however, I would not want people to conclude "Well, I'm not the type to be able to lead such a moral life, so wouldn't it be rather impertinent to think like that?" Human beings are all the same. From God's viewpoint, none are without sin. It is merely the difference between those who do something wrong through a stroke of fate and those who are protected by something, so that they get by okay despite thinking bad thoughts.

In order for such weak human beings to somehow manage to live together, we need to forge morals for our technology-mediated environment. If matters are left alone, there's no knowing what evil might be unleashed. And we need to protect these morals. If we think we are bad or weak, all the more reason to think about morals. It could be argued that morals exist as a measure of our own iniquity. It is only when we have a barometer of iniquity that we start to feel motivated to crawl out of this iniquity even a little.

Although I am writing about morals, by no means can I boast that my own morals and ethics are superior to those of other people. If pressed, I would have to admit to a multitude of flaws. But we all know this without being told—so we can forgive each other.

Yet if mutual forgiveness meant besmirching each other, that would be unacceptable. That is not how things should turn out. Somewhere in mutual forgiveness lie the bonds of morality, as something affording a glimpse of the human race's future, something whereby we draw closer to our aspirations. Even though we ourselves might not be able to abide by these moral precepts, I would like us to dwell in hope by looking to morals as an important ideal, a goal the striving toward which contributes even a little to the happiness of the human race and to becoming even a slightly better person oneself. *Eco-ethica* can be posited as that bond.

Let's revisit the concept of the three houses across the road and the houses on each side. "Across the road" doesn't apply in the case of condominiums and apartments, and instead the neighbours on each side and above and below take on importance. One fundamental reason for this is the question of noise, which had never been an ethical issue in the past. The situations in which human beings can make noises vocally are fixed, so there was no likelihood of calling out right into the night, and noise never really became an ethical issue.

Recently, however, noise has become a problem, even giving rise to the expression 'soundscape'. This is because various media emit highly unpleasant or loud noises as well as sounds such as low-frequency waves that produce various psychological effects. If we close our eyes, we can avoid looking at things we don't want to see, but it is physiologically impossible to close our ears, unless we use some device. Nowadays noise has become something that threatens human freedom from multiple directions, so not bothering others with noise needs to be established as a moral principle. This is an issue that has emerged since society became a technological society and noise-emitting media proliferated and an environment arose where we make noise when working. This issue is particularly important for people with a visual impairment.

Today there are many such problems, but in this chapter I have restricted the discussion to issues relating to contemporary culture. In closing, let me stress that there are many issues requiring the formulation of a new ethics, so there is a need for ethics to be reinstated. It is absolutely essential for us to formulate a new ethics. Toward that end, I ask not just my fellow researchers involved in the academic study of ethics, but also those on the 'front line' who are actually confronting a range of ethical issues to assist in various ways, such as pooling their concerns and sharing and debating views from a range of specialized fields, as well as their ideas as citizens. At that time, however, I don't want people to think that ethics can be dealt with simply by establishing codes of practice and work regulations. Although comments by ethicists with no knowledge of a particular occupation will have little impact on the code of practice for a restricted occupation, codes of practice and work regulations need to be based on ethics, and in themselves these do not yet constitute ethics.

The most concrete characteristic of ethics lies in virtues. What kinds of virtues are conceivable as *eco-ethica* virtues? The next chapter will explore this question.

NOTES

1. This work, which was published by Iwanami Shoten in 1931, has been translated into English by Seisaku Yamamoto and Robert E. Carter as *Rinrigaku* (Albany: State University of New York Press, 1996).—Trans.

2. These words have been attributed to the Meiji-era politician Taisuke Itagaki (1837–1919), a leader in the People's Freedom and Rights Movement, when a fanatic attempted to assassinate him in Gifu in 1882.—Trans.

Chapter Three

A New Virtue Ethics

VIRTUES AS THE SPECIFIC MANIFESTATION OF AN ETHICAL SYSTEM

It is difficult to give an appropriate definition of the nature of virtue. Even the important dialogue *Meno*, where Plato recognizes the existence of Ideas, starts out from virtue and returns to this question. That demonstrates the complexity of this concept, yet it certainly does not mean that anyone is unaware of what virtue is. It is a universally understood concept. And as mentioned at the end of the previous chapter, what reveals a system of ethics most specifically is the hierarchy of virtues espoused by that system. For instance, citing the five cardinal virtues of Confucianism—benevolence, justice, politeness, wisdom and fidelity—offers a general idea of what kind of ethics Confucianism represents, and the four cardinal virtues described by Aristotle—justice, courage, wisdom and moderation—give a general picture of the ethics of the polises (city-states) of ancient Greece. What were regarded as virtues among Japanese military groups and right-wing ideologues as Japan headed into World War II—i.e., loyalty and patriotism and dying for one's country—made even us young people at the time realize that this was an insular and nationalistic ethics far different from the ethics of Christianity, with its advocacy of love for humankind. I might add that Christian ethics regards faith, hope and love as the most important virtues. Demonstrating the kind of virtues advocated by *eco-ethica*, therefore, will provide an even clearer picture of *eco-ethica* than that presented so far.

Eco-ethica is a new ethics, but this does not mean it needs to reinvent from scratch all the virtues that are important to human beings. *Eco-ethica* adopts many virtues from existing ethics, while also creating some anew—otherwise it would not be able to present itself as a new ethics. Although ethics does not consist solely of virtue ethics (aretology), an ethical system is revealed most concretely in its theory of virtues.

Yet is it actually possible to create new virtues? Morals and ethics have endured through people passing down the virtues that the human race has possessed since of old, and we could even argue that in fact the world has become modern by *reducing* the number of virtues. For instance, when an emperor died in ancient Asia it was customary for his retainers to follow him to the grave, and this was regarded as an act of outstanding virtue. One of the most recent examples of this custom, known as *junshi* in Japan, was the ritual suicides of General Maresuke Nogi and his wife on the day of Emperor Meiji's funeral, out of a desire to follow their lord in death. Such acts, however, negate the uniqueness of an individual's existence, and with exceptions such as General Nogi, where these acts are truly carried out through one's own resolve and mental preparedness, these acts are utterly atrocious if they are the result of coercion. That is why in olden times *junshi* was originally forbidden in Japan too. The burial mound figures of ancient Japan are thought to be funerary goods that were intended to function as substitutes for human retainers. So virtues might be abolished in this way, but surely no new virtues are created? Ethics presumably represents the voice of the elders who tried to maintain laudable ancient customs as much as possible. Yet is that really so?

THE HISTORY OF CREATING VIRTUES

To me, the history of ethics is a history of revolution. For example, in his masterpiece *Politia* (*The Republic*) the great philosopher Plato proposed abolishing the family as an institution. In the long run his proposal was not adopted in that form, but to this very day children spend a great deal of time outside the home (e.g., at school, in dormitories, or away on trips). What does this signify? If we value the family on the grounds that parental love is absolutely essential for children as they are growing up, what about those who are misfortunate enough to lose their parents? Although such children are indeed disadvantaged, the fact that they still grow up properly suggests that the meaning of the family lies elsewhere. The importance of love between husband and wife is another rationale for the family, but in reality there are married couples who would end up killing or injuring each other if they did not obtain a divorce. There is also the social violence involved in marriage.

One example of social violence in the home is the fact that since olden times there has been a tendency to label illegitimate children and unjustly shun them from society, despite the fact that they have not sinned. This attitude has been particularly strong among the so-called bourgeoisie. Up until about 1930 or 1940 there were moves in Japan to indicate a baby's illegitimate status on the family register and to drop illegitimate candidates out of the running for jobs. In a sense this could be described as a kind of familial violence enacted by society. Another example is the suffering endured by children whose parents have unfortunately died. Such situations have led some countries to try out schemes in line with the Platonic ideal, whereby children are educated and raised communally on kibbutzes.

If we were truly prepared to love others and look after them and if there were guarantees to that effect in place, such issues would probably not present a major problem, but placing value on the family also has the negative aspect that it benefits only those who belong to a complete family. So the egoism of the family will continue to attract criticism. We also need to formulate ethics on the assumption that the institution of the family might disappear.

Even though Japan is not a socialist country, in some respects policies of state socialism are even more widespread there than in socialist countries, and not much wealth is preserved for the next generation. Despite certain inequities, there has been a gradual disappearance of families whose offspring are born into great wealth and do not need to earn a living. Conversely, it is relatively unusual to be born so poor that one cannot attend school. In short, we have realized that social discrimination on family grounds, such as the familial violence mentioned above, can be prevented to some extent through social policies, so some people believe there is no need to be as radical as Plato.

I have given ongoing serious thought to such matters, however, and though I might be mistaken, I believe that unless we pool various theories and formulate some kind of moral guidelines at the academic level, ethics will become completely ineffective both in education and in actual life, so that it will inevitably be regarded as a mere shadow of its former self.

From the perspective of ethics, it seems to me that philosophy underwent a complete transformation after Nietzsche, Marx and Freud. Nietzsche rejected naïve faith and proclaimed that "God is dead"—i.e., he demonstrated the need for a morality independent of faith. Marx questioned why class-based discrimination is overlooked and why society can get away with exploiting its hard-working labourers—i.e., he raised the questions of justice and liberation. Freud asked why society does not give serious consideration to morality in relation to sex, which is a vital issue for human beings. All three topics are deeply imbricated with the question of the family. There are various ongoing efforts in connection with the issues raised by these three thinkers, but we have not yet reached a stage where we can respond adequately in moral terms. It must also be acknowledged that neither these thinkers nor their followers have taken responsibility for the extent to which these questions plunged morals into confusion. If we take the view that such realities exist as a major problem, then an awareness of the need for new virtues naturally arises.

In that case, the question is whether such revolutionary ideas can be formulated in relation to human morals. Keep in mind that major revolutionary changes in ethics also occurred as religious issues during the transition from Old Testament to New Testament times. The teaching of the Old Testament—the idea that divine salvation pertains to one people chosen by God—is of course a fine teaching. In line with this, the people of Israel believed that they would attain salvation through being chosen by God. The New Testament, however, developed this further so that divine salvation extends to the entire human race. This can be summed up in terms of the transition from a god of justice to a god of love, but ultimately it means that divine salvation does not occur through blood ties or legal ties. It is the outcome of a covenant bond. Regardless of birth or nation, one has the potential for salvation through the covenant bond. Of course this was a religious matter, but it also strengthened morals, which firmly promote the idea of equality among individuals.

There are several historical figures to whose perspective and powers of thought I can truly doff my philosopher's hat. Nietzsche is one. But if I had to choose a single such figure, it would be Plato. Regrettably, however, even Plato adopted a position that justified slavery. As perhaps suggested by the expression 'institution of slavery', in this context 'slavery' might not necessarily refer to the atrocious treatment of slaves, but to the inequitable system whereby citizenship or lack thereof is determined by birth. This is something that no ethicists or philosophers have supported since New Testament times. The fact that Plato, who was critical of the family on the grounds that it was a source of inequality and imperfection among citizens, failed to realize this and was unable to adopt a viewpoint encompassing the whole human race represents a major contradiction. Nevertheless, the universalism of Christianity, whose realization of this led to the emancipation of slaves, is a fine demonstration of the major role played by religion in ethics. Regardless of whether or not one holds Christian beliefs, the fact that we are all equal before God can be viewed as the foundation of ethics.

This means that issues raised from a religious perspective have also been fully acknowledged in the fields of moral science and ethics. Post-New Testament ethics was accordingly encouraged to develop on the premise that all people are equal in moral fibre. So philosophers have long arrayed themselves against any undue discrimination carried out in the name of the law, no matter how much lawyers and policymakers might regard them as a thorn in the side. This opposition to discrimination is based on the fact that in purely ethical terms human beings are of equal moral character. It's just that they differ in personality, which is the historical outgrowth of their moral character.

We must also recognize that major revolutions in awareness have likewise occurred in the domain of ethics over the course of human history. The words *morals* and *ethics* inevitably conjure up images of fusty moral scientists, and people are apt to think that they will peddle morals and commandments. Since some old morals are of course good ones, it would be mistaken to simply advocate a wholesale overhaul. Nevertheless, we should not forget that ethics has also made revolutionary progress, so let's use that as one guideline for considering the situation today.

(1) Courage

I suggest, then, that a new environment calls for the development of new virtues. Yet is it really possible to create virtues? Can the meaning of existing virtues truly undergo a transformation?

A response to these questions can be found by considering the original meaning of the contemporary word *virtue*. This derives from the Latin word *virtus*, which took on various forms in different languages. In Latin *vir* means a man, and *virtus* means manliness, which came to take on the additional meaning of virtue. Why was manliness valued as a virtue in the West in ancient times? First, remember the barbaric conditions prevailing in primitive times. People had no idea when or where an enemy might attack, but these attacks were bound to be instigated by men from outside, armed with spears and swords, bows and arrows. Again, at such times it was men who would defend the community. They would risk their lives to protect their wives, children and the elderly, as well as the village's property and the village clan. This attitude and such actions are what constituted manliness. It is only natural that a man who gave his blood and life to save his kin would be described as full of manliness. And this manliness—*virtus*—is esteemed as an act of virtue. This is because this person's courage—i.e., his willingness even to die—resulted in protecting the village and achieving victory. Again, with the Japanese word for *courage* (*yūki* 勇気), the first character consists in part of the character for *man* (*otoko* 男), again emphasizing manliness. A similar situation existed in China in olden times, which is only natural, since there too it was impossible to defend a village unless one truly fought with all one's physical might. So courage—i.e., manliness—was held in great esteem.

This old-world virtue did not lose currency once society and culture evolved and killing was no longer an everyday act. Instead the word *manliness* came to refer to the possession of courage—not just the courage of men in combat, but internal fortitude, be that on the part of a man or a woman. For instance, suppose a woman's husband has been killed by enemy soldiers. When she protects her child, who is all that remains to her, and stands tall no matter how tough life might be, she represents the epitome of motherhood and womanhood and is lauded for her courage in overcoming so many difficulties. Here the character *yū* (勇 courage) takes on a different sense from manliness through mere physical strength, referring instead to the mental strength that all human beings possess, regardless of gender. Today when we say "Have courage" to someone, male or female, sometimes their faith is being questioned. Those who bow to authority and abandon their faith and beliefs are said to lack courage, regardless of their gender. No matter how physically strong a man might be, if power or wealth, for instance, induce him to change his beliefs, he must be regarded as lacking in courage.

Since courage has been internalized in this way and the term is used irrespective of gender, today nobody translates the word *virtue* into Japanese using the word for *manliness* (*otoko-rashisa* 男らしさ; literally, the quality of being like a man). Instead it is translated as *toku* 徳, the standard word today for virtue. And *yūki* (courage) is something that not only men but also women should possess. It is not that a new word was coined, but that the meaning of an existing word shifted and deepened—i.e., a semantic transformation occurred. This must be regarded as progress in ethics and morals.

Who says progress happens only in the realm of science? When people make comments to that effect, I sometimes wonder whether I'm being regarded as an idler because I am a philosopher. Good things stand the test of time. In that sense, the situation is different from in science, where the old is always regarded as outdated. Science is constantly advancing, but evolution in the arts and philosophy is much less rapid. Nevertheless, things that are new and good are bound to emerge. Since both philosophy and ethics are academic disciplines, scholarly efforts should lead to progress. My point here, however, is that the above example illustrates not the coining of a new word or expression, but the imparting of new content to an existing word, and that this is how progress in morals has occurred.

(2) Loyalty

As a very similar example, let us look at the East Asian concept of loyalty. Here there are ups and downs—progress and regression—in this concept.

What constituted loyalty in the past, in the Edo days of feudal lords? As depicted in the *Chūshingura* (a famous tale celebrating the loyal sacrifice of 47 *rōnin* or leaderless samurai in the eighteenth century), this entailed absolute fealty to one's master. If someone from another domain insulted one's lord, it was acceptable to kill that person—even a fellow countryman—in the name of loyalty. I can identify with the anger on the part of the *Chūshingura*'s Lord Takuminokami Asano, who was forced to commit ritual suicide after assaulting a court official who had insulted him. When I hear of contemporary incidents such as the Recruit influence-peddling scandal, where politics was swayed by bribes, and when I hear that even elections, the cornerstone of democratic politics, can be more easily won by collecting off-the-book funds and buying votes, I fully understand Takuminokami's anger. I also understand full well the feelings of the 47 *rōnin* led by Kuranosuke Ōishi. In terms of contemporary social norms, however, we must ultimately conclude that Kuranosuke's attitude involved ganging up with the other *rōnin* and conspiring to commit murder in revenge for their master's death. If we look at this from the perspective of the somewhat improved state of morals today compared with early modern times, we realize that the virtue of loyalty in those days involved giving one's all to the lord of a single domain, and we are forced to consider whether this is acceptable.

After the Meiji Restoration of 1868 this concept of loyalty in Japan—as was the case with advanced nations at that time—was transformed into loyalty toward the state, the entire nation, or the emperor, as the sovereign ruler of the nation. This represents a clear improvement over the concept of loyalty whereby people from different domains would kill each other, even if both parties were Japanese. Nevertheless, surely even today nobody would deem it acceptable to kill people of another nationality in the name of loyalty when problems arise between nations or peoples. The idea of coexistence can be found in just about every country. And the virtue of loyalty—i.e., fealty and faithfulness—is now regarded as referring to being a loyal citizen or working dutifully for one's organization (e.g., a company or school), or to loyalty to one's superiors and friends. This shows just how much the virtue of loyalty has been revamped over the past century or half-century compared with the concept of loyalty that prevailed three or four centuries ago.

Yet the modernization of virtues does not necessarily mean that the more recent a virtue, the more superior it is. That is why we need to be aware and conduct ourselves in a disciplined manner in any period. Let us look at this in more specific terms.

What did people have in mind when this concept of loyalty was first formulated? This virtue appears in the *Analects* of Confucius, where Zengzi, one of his leading disciples, discusses loyalty as follows: "I examine myself three times a day: In dealing with others, have I been disloyal?" Here loyalty to "others" does not mean loyalty to those above one, such as superiors or the organization to which one belongs. Instead, this is a very human concept that involves the need to interact with any and all others from the bottom of one's heart—i.e., reflecting on whether one is acting in good faith. So in Confucius's day loyalty was conceived of as the attitude of interacting wholeheartedly with all others, be they one's superiors, one's peers or those of lower rank, or be they of a different ethnicity. Hence a sense of interpersonal integrity and interpersonal sincerity was the original hallmark of loyalty.

Over the years this concept underwent various changes, for better and for worse, right up to the present. So there was an earlier concept of loyalty created by some anonymous person, and then there was a moral leap and progress when Confucius first formulated the concept of loyalty as a clear virtue. At one stage this was exploited by feudal lords and by kept scholars. When the concept became even narrower it was reduced to loyalty to a small organization, with even fellow countrymen killing each other. And today things are different again, with loyalty being directed toward civil society.

Even if we limit our analysis to the Japanese concept of loyalty, it is apparent then that morals and virtues are by no means conservative—they carry a history of changes for the better and the worse. Nevertheless, we need to reclaim the original meaning of loyalty. We need to go back to square one and consider loyalty as an internal criterion of sincerity as to whether we are interacting sincerely with other people, be they our superiors, our peers, those of lower rank, or strangers. My comments about the Japanese concept of loyalty are more or less equally applicable, for example, to the English word *loyalty*.

Yet perhaps we should expand the scope of loyalty further and also interact with cultural assets and the environment with a loyal and sincere attitude. We need to consider whether the term *loyalty* can be used in relation to non-human entities. There is much talk these days about chlorofluorocarbons. Is it acceptable for us to destroy the natural balance on earth for our own convenience? If we do, what will happen to future generations and other life forms? Such reflections make it abundantly clear that through loyalty we must bear responsibility to many entities. I will return to this question of responsibility later, and at that time we must keep in mind that what we are considering here is the issue of whether morals can be created.

(3) Humility

A long time ago a completely new term was coined in the field of morality. The coining of a new term signifies that a new concept has been discovered or invented. I'm sure readers have heard that we should all be humble, and they would no doubt agree that humility is important. In reality, arrogance disqualifies one from scholarship. It is difficult to set aside our arrogance, but we cannot engage in scholarship unless we are aware that we are far from the truth and unless we look up to outstanding works and try to find something to learn from in the words of others. In that sense I believe that one of the virtues necessary in our work is humility. Although there is nothing so distasteful as false humility, fundamentally we need to be humble.

Morals have existed from of old, so we would expect the key term *humility* to appear in all books on ethics, but that is not so. *Megalopsychia* (magnanimity), which signifies pride and greatness of soul, is cited as an important virtue in Aristotle's famous *Nicomachean Ethics*. Yet nowhere in any works in Classical Greek is there a word corresponding to humility.

So when did this come into being? The first occurrence is the word *tapeinophrosune*, which appears, for example, in Ephesians in the New Testament and in the apocryphal Teachings of the Twelve Apostles (The Didache). The word *tapeinos* was an adjective meaning 'lowly', and *phrosune* could be rendered as 'thinking'. In Greece *tapeinos* referred to the characteristics of *ptochos* (beggars). So *tapeinophrosune* meant the attitude of a beggar. In ancient Greece nobody was looked down upon as much as the itinerant beggars who received leftover food from people. Just recall Homer's *Odyssey* or the tales of Homer. When Odysseus tried to creep into his own home as unobtrusively as possible, he adopted the guise of a beggar. Nobody would pay any attention to a beggar, so he could return home without being noticed. In ancient Greece beggars were regarded as trash, lower than dogs, so their presence was of no account. Without work, they could not even be a slave—that's how disdained they were.

Conversely, what was regarded as a virtue in Greece, as a desirable attribute for Greek citizens, was *megalopsychia*—i.e., a large heart, an open heart, a generous heart, where one thrust out one's chest proudly when walking. *Tapeinophrosune*, a self-abased heart, was the diametric opposite of this. As noted above, the word *tapeinophrosune* appears in one of Paul's letters and was assumedly a crystallization of the thought of Christ, who advocated a lowly attitude like that of a beggar. This teaching appears in the Sermon on the Mount: "Blessed are the poor in spirit". In the original Greek "poor in spirit" is the colourful expression "beggars [*ptochos*] in spirit", which is a literal translation of what Christ said in Aramaic.

Beggars do not adopt the attitude of asking for alms and pulling their hand back if someone gives them only a small amount, while accepting the money if it's a larger amount. If they are not grateful for any amount, no matter how small it might be, they are not genuine beggars in dire need. So if one only reaches out for the good fortune bestowed by God and not for the ordeals he ordains, one is not truly a child of God. An attitude of stretching out one's hand like a beggar and regarding everything from God as a blessing, no matter what it might be—that is the true meaning of "Blessed are the poor in spirit".

From this feeling of receiving whatever people bestow, no matter what that might be, derives the *tapeinophrosune* that lies at the root of the concept of humility. And ever since this word was coined, no catalogues of virtue in medieval Christian ethics have excluded humility. It has become a full-fledged virtue. We should remember, however, that this virtue of humility or modesty was first created in the Western world by followers of Christianity. Naturally, even without this being posited as a virtue, a corresponding attitude and behaviour did of course exist, but until Christianity was founded it was not regarded as an ethical virtue at all. The abolition of the institution of slavery is also no doubt related to this.

(4) Responsibility

People are smart today, and in their actual lives they obey institutions and customs, behaving in a way that will not be to their detriment and will not result in legal sanctions. As a result, many people think ethics are outdated, so they no longer hold out any hopes for new virtues. They believe that even if we were to try, it would be impossible to come up with new virtues. Human beings are not all that philosophical; if anything, we are technologically minded, so instead of doing things like creating virtues, all that's necessary is to improve technology—or so goes their thinking.

Yet even with the modern advent of science and technology, virtues are indeed being created. For instance, responsibility is an indispensable concept that underpins moral life in both the West and Japan. It is not generally known how long responsibility has been under discussion in the West, so we need to peruse the literature and determine when this word first came into use. It turns out, however, that this means considering the fact that a creative evolution has occurred in relation to responsibility—an evolution that was not steered by religion, but occurred in purely ethical terms.

One contemporary philosophical movement is that known as existentialism. This focuses on the individual's existence—the existence of the self—and values the signs of one's existence as an individual, rather than stressing the human essence, as had been the case in the past. One scholar holding such a view was F. H. Heinemann. Emulating Descartes' "Cogito, ergo sum" (I think, therefore I am)—I'm sure readers have heard of this statement—Heinemann wrote "Respondeo, ergo sum". Literally, this means "I respond [to someone], therefore I am". What it implies is that "I have a responsibility to respond to someone, and that is the proof of my existence." The idea here is that I have a responsibility, so I exist. This sees the significance of self-existence—the proof of self-existence—not in 'thinking', but in 'awareness of responsibility', which indicates how important the concept or virtue of responsibility has become in modern society.

Nevertheless, as I have demonstrated elsewhere, we must remember that responsibility is a virtue created in early modern times. Let us delve into the background from which this virtue must have emerged.

Since this is a word that readers are bound to have learnt in school, it must have been in existence in the twentieth century. It was also around in the nineteenth century. I realized that it first appeared in a work published at the end of the eighteenth century—specifically, in 1778. Along with the French word *responsabilité* and the German *Verantwortung*, this important word *responsibility*—which today we all regard as an accepted social norm and use in expressions such as "You need to act with responsibility" or "This accident was caused by a lack of responsibility" and on a daily basis as a moral term—did not exist before the latter half of the eighteenth century.

This hypothesis that I presented back in 1956—the same year as Richard McKeon—has still not been refuted, which suggests that before 1778 the word *responsibility* did not exist. The lack of such a word does not, however, mean that responsible behaviour was non-existent in the West in olden times. Even if unacquainted with this actual word, people such as Socrates and Christians such as Sebastian all exhibited responsibility. Socrates believed that his way of life lay in obeying the law, which constituted a 'contract' with the city-state, and so he accepted without demur the legal pronouncement that he be sentenced to death. Rejecting advice to escape by paying off his jailers, he was put to death. And Sebastian became a martyr because his death demonstrated his devotion to the Lord Jesus Christ. So a sense of responsibility did exist, but this concept did not yet exist as a virtue.

The subsequent conceptualization of responsibility was linked to the fact that large-scale transportation of materials became feasible when science and technology began to be put to practical uses in the days of James Watt—i.e., right in the latter half of the eighteenth century. When as a result bartering disappeared and contract societies built on reciprocal agreement came into existence even for commodity transactions, the idea arose that acting in accordance with a covenant with the other party and responding to each other—even without any goods physically present—are important basic attitudes that are absolutely indispensable for the performance of a contract. The word *responsibility* is derived from the music term *response*, which originated in the medieval practice whereby members of a choir known as a responsorium would line up in two facing rows, each of which would take turns singing in response to the other. As noted earlier, the word *responsibility* was coined for the first time in the eighteenth century.

The German word *Verantwortung* did not appear until the nineteenth century. So no amount of searching will turn up this word anywhere in Immanuel Kant's *Kritik der praktischen Vernunft* (*Critique of Practical Reason*), which is regarded as a major work on ethics. Although the philosophy dictionaries that supposedly contain the key concepts in ethics (the famous nineteenth-century dictionary edited by the German Rudolf

Eisler and the dictionary compiled by the French scholar André Lalande) purportedly represent the finest of their countries' cultures, the French word *responsabilité* does not appear in the first editions of these works, and nor does the corresponding German word *Verantwortlichkeit*. They were added when revised editions were published in the twentieth century, and with each new edition the explanations have become a little more elaborate, so that nowadays any dictionary one might care to check contains a detailed entry of at least a page for this concept. The fact that responsibility—a truly vital moral concept in modern European societies, and one that also seems important for Japanese society—appeared for the first time in the eighteenth century, at least in the West, and that it was not until the twentieth century that people really became aware of this concept shows that human beings are capable of creating revolutionary new virtues in the sweep of history.

Living in our present times of technological innovation, we must together create some new values. So who is going to do this? Can it really be left up to some philosopher, ethicist or sociologist? It is true that we scholars of ethics do bear this responsibility, but what is important is not the creativity of individuals, but of the human race as a whole. The reason I say this is that, amazingly enough, we still do not know who coined the word for this virtue of responsibility. When I gave my presentation back in 1956, I said it was important to determine who coined this word, so I asked the foreign academics in attendance to cooperate as much as possible in finding out the answer to this question. According to Richard McKeon, apparently the word was first used in a work by John Stuart Mill but was not in fact coined by him. We still don't know the originator of this word, although no doubt we will eventually find out one day. Nevertheless, this individual's long-standing anonymity suggests that the term emerged as the product of a communal consciousness.

It would be mistaken to regard the creation of such moral concepts as a phenomenon unique to the West, as many such cases can be found in Japan as well. New moral concepts have been formulated in each period of Japanese history. Examples would include filial piety and the abovementioned changes in *bushidō* loyalty. The *wabi* (reclusiveness) of hermits and the *iki* (a particular blend of stylishness and sophistication) of people on the street also became virtues that have been discovered as moral concepts, since they relate to how we live our lives. And although some say this word is now obsolete, a further example would be *mottainasa* (frugality) as a virtue in relation to things, since this word does not occur in old documents such as the *Kojiki*, but was created at a later point in time.

So the feeling that we need to look after things and appreciate them should be regarded as embodying a grass-roots movement. Readers of this book are intellectuals—i.e., an elite—by virtue of the fact that they are reading a work of this nature. Society naturally requires members of the elite to take pride in their work and carry it out responsibly, but it would be mistaken to believe that the elite are capable of guiding the public in all matters. A grass-roots movement that also includes the elite from each field is important when changing the meaning of virtues or creating new virtues, and this is not something that should be done by only a handful of elite people. Surely the fact that our society is regarded as a knowledge society signifies that all members of the public are part of the elite in their own particular field. In that sense, the elite is broadening, so an intellectual ethics might be expected to take root.

THE CREATION OF NEW VIRTUES

(1) *Philoxenia* (love of strangers)

One of the virtues that are very gradually emerging in Japan and elsewhere is kindness toward foreigners. Although even today not all Japanese transport facilities (with the exception of railway station names) are 'user-friendly', in that the signs are written only in Japanese, a trend toward using romanized Japanese in signs has begun to appear. Public institutions unconsciously focus only on people who have much in common with most of the public. At most Japanese railway stations, for instance, there are a lot of stairs, so people in wheelchairs cannot use them, and people who are blind and foreigners unable to read Japanese cannot even purchase a ticket. And it's not just at railway stations. A similar situation sometimes applies to the signs on expressways and at ordinary government offices and companies. So it is up to society as a whole to extend a helping hand to foreigners.

I'm not sure how to describe this. Perhaps it could be termed neighbourly love, but in reference to foreigners in particular I will use the term *philoxenia*, which means kindness to strangers. Even in Japan, a particularly closed society, it seems that kindness toward foreigners is making its appearance a little. Nevertheless, children of mixed race are sometimes bullied at school simply because the colour of their hair is different—even though they are Japanese. So there is a need for efforts to make *philoxenia* take firm root in society.

In the light of the above, I believe we can indeed say that a new virtue is in the making. If we look back on incidents such as that in Kanagawa over a century ago when four British citizens were attacked by xenophobic followers of a feudal lord, we must conclude that the Japanese have become far more open and caring. Although at the time of the Meiji Restoration people did indeed think it was acceptable to kill people who were different or unusual-looking, today we no longer take that view. This is a reflection of the emergence of the virtue of *philoxenia* around the world, including Japan.

(2) Punctuality

One new virtue that has become widespread in our technology-mediated environment is punctiliousness or, to put it another way, punctuality. Various unfortunate, detrimental and inconvenient consequences occur in society if people are not punctual. When machines are involved, we need to be on time. If trains are not operating on schedule, it would be easy for a train that was late leaving the station to crash into the train that departed ahead of it.

In the past, invitations would say "At six sharp", meaning that arriving late would be a problem. Nowadays nobody uses that expression any more. If the invitation says "Six o'clock", the event will generally start at six. From today's vantage point it is clear that in the old days people thought that being overly punctilious about time was a sign of servitude. Important people didn't worry if they were five or ten minutes late. And truly important people would arrive an hour late. Today, however, it would be out of the question to hold events on that basis. Nowadays all meetings and gatherings of any kind are held pretty much on schedule, out of consideration for those who have come from afar and out of a sense of respect for everyone's time. This shows that punctuality has joined the catalogue of ethical virtues.

In the past, punctuality referred solely to adhering strictly to the correct time. Alongside this, however, today *ponctualité* (punctiliousness) refers to accuracy in pressing the correct buttons when operating machinery. In our technology-mediated environment, when pushing the wrong button can lead to a fatal accident, punctiliousness or precision also becomes an important virtue in terms of work ethics. Since this strict attention to detail might demean people, however, we need to think of a counterbalancing virtue. I would like to reinstate *eutrapelia* (mental diversion) as a virtue, and I will touch on this below.

(3) Cosmopolitanism

Cosmopolitanism in the true sense of the term has, I believe, made its way into the realm of morals as another new virtue. Readers might wonder whether this attribute constitutes a moral virtue, but stressing cosmopolitanism is an ethically important task.

Let me share with you a disturbing anecdote that illustrates how things were in Tokyo up until about a decade ago. It is about a little girl who had what is commonly referred to as mixed parentage. In an attempt to conform to Japanese customs as much as possible, her parents enrolled her in a local Buddhist kindergarten. Pigeons would often come and leave droppings on the balcony of their place. One day, shortly after the little girl entered kindergarten, she was clapping her hands vigorously to chase the pigeons away. I happened to be there at the time. With no idea of the meaning of her words, the girl, who was three at the time, was shouting out "Go away, foreigners!". At that, the pigeons flew off. So she said "Daddy, this is fun. When I say that word they use at kindergarten, the pigeons fly away." Her father laughed, but I felt a bit bad or sorry on her behalf. When I asked how she learned that word, she said "When I'm playing in the sandpit, boys come up to me and say "Go away, foreigner!" And when that happens I have to leave straight away." This little girl was unfamiliar with the word *foreigner*, so apparently she did not particularly feel discriminated against, but many other children have ended up in tears because of such name-calling.

So how do things stand now, fifteen years later? I doubt if that sort of incident happens much at kindergartens these days. International understanding—i.e., the idea that even if the colour of someone's hair and skin differs from your own, you can still become friends because you are both human beings—has developed even among children. The world makes great strides in the space of just ten or fifteen years. The degree of cosmopolitanism also determines the likelihood of trade friction.

I believe that young people are gradually abandoning the attitudes I'm about to describe now, but when I occasionally travel overseas to give a talk at a foreign university, I often come across the following scenes. Apparently Japanese visitors to places such as Paris, Dusseldorf and Amsterdam can take Japanese currency with them and return home without having spent any other currency overseas. For instance, a restaurant that serves great Japanese food opens in a certain city in northern Europe. When you go there, the waiters, who are Japanese, are very polite, and there is a menu of appetizing Japanese dishes. Customers are told that they are welcome to pay in yen. Since having the prices listed in yen makes it easier to get an idea of the cost, the customers end up paying in yen.

All this is fair enough. But when you say "I'd like to buy such-and-such at a souvenir shop. Can you recommend somewhere?", you're told that a certain Japanese-operated store has a full range of souvenirs from Scandinavian countries. Since you don't speak any Scandinavian languages, you decide to visit this store. On arrival you find that even that country's flags that are sold there carry a "Made in Japan" label. This is something a friend of mine who lives in that city told me. Things are arranged so that a solely Japanese clientele spends vast sums of Japanese money at a Japanese-owned store and the only people to make a profit are the Japanese. I too thought this setup would make life easier, but then I realized there's something wrong with this, so I changed my mind and sought out for myself a shop selling Scandinavian specialties, where I came across an unusual large notebook with a cover made of wood.

My friend told me that all of this means the locals make no money even with lots of Japanese tourists visiting. The tourists are taken around by escorts and tour guides who accompanied them from Japan, and they buy their souvenirs at Japanese-owned shops. If they're hungry, they eat at Japanese-owned restaurants. Paying in yen is no problem. So they don't spend any money at locally owned stores, and they even buy all their souvenirs at stores operated by Japanese. That's why the locals prefer even Americans. Americans don't act like that. Generally speaking, they are truly easy-going. Even if they are ripped off at a dodgy antique dealer's store when visiting Japan, they still cough up the money. And since they're in Japan, they are interested, presumably out of curiosity, in eating Japanese food, and they spend money at Japanese-operated restaurants instead of going to an American-operated steak house.

Today the Japanese are acting abroad in the same way as did the Occupation forces, who used to shop at American-operated military stores called a PX and pay in dollars. The Japanese are carrying out an *economic* occupation, so there's every reason for them to be hated. Nowadays some Japanese buy up historic old castles in Germany or France and make a profit by turning them into contemporary-style hotels, much to the chagrin of Europeans. Such actions lay the way for even normal economic competition to be misconstrued.

Cosmopolitanism originally consisted of profound preparations aimed at avoiding war. Once someone hates you, inevitably war becomes a strong likelihood. So although avoiding war is more than just a matter of individual conviction, we need to think long and hard about the meaning of cosmopolitanism or internationalism. It is a question of mental attitude—i.e., an issue of ethics—not a matter of being able to speak a foreign language.

(4) Mastery of languages and equipment

Since the state system is likely to remain a powerful institution for some time to come, internationalism needs to be fostered as an important virtue, but in future cosmopolitanism should be formulated as an even more important virtue that transcends internationalism. In the time of Hellenism this concept was mainly advocated by the Stoic philosophers, using the neologism *kosmopolites* (citizen of the world), and subsequently it was also valued in Christian circles. For instance, godfathers were classified not on the basis of nationality or race, for example, but according to the language they used—Greek godfather, Latin godfather, Coptic godfather, Syrian godfather and so on. The eighteenth century was another time when people had a strong awareness of cosmopolitanism in the sense of being a citizen of the world (*Weltbürger*), particularly through Kant's influence. In the twenty-first century a member of our research group, Peter Kemp, has advocated cosmopolitanism as one of the most vital virtues, while Marco Olivetti has stated that the foundation of cosmopolitanism lies in respecting others as an individual, regardless of any collateral conditions. In this respect, Kant remains an important figure in terms of ethics, as Joseph Simon has argued. The statements of Paul Ricœur, who proposed ipseity (selfhood) in relation to others, are also important.

Nevertheless, a command of foreign languages is indeed necessary, not from the perspective of making a profit for oneself, but so as to be able to interact with others. Based on an attitude of interacting ethically with people and helping them, mastery of at least one foreign language represents a new virtue in society today, as a manifestation of cosmopolitanism. I believe this constitutes an intellectual virtue.

And since we live in a technological society, it is important to be able to operate at least one piece of equipment. This too becomes a virtue. The ability to drive a car means the ability to make life easier for others—for instance, by taking sick or elderly people to hospital—so in that sense it is important to be proactive in acquiring technical skills, although there is no need to be enslaved by technology. These skills are on a par with the need to be able to swim in nature.

Being highly cosmopolitan is particularly critical. It is my belief that one day a borderless world will come into being. *Eco-ethica* exists for that purpose. It leads to the idea that all human beings are equal in terms of moral character. *Eco-ethica* could be regarded as a manifestation of that hope.

Perhaps anyone could come up with these ideas as plain common sense, but I am pushing to consider them as a theoretical system—i.e., ethics or philosophy. This is, however, a difficult task, and even at universities there are no facilities for studying such topics, so we need help in carrying out such research. One form of assistance involves gradually widening the circle of people who are reflecting on and discussing these topics. These books of mine will sell and be read if people think that they will contribute even slightly to the future of the human race and will help widen the circle. If that happens, the concepts of this new ethics on which we are pinning our hopes for the future will permeate the public consciousness. It is only when individuals, one by one, put their minds to such matters that *eco-ethica* will come into being.

(5) *Eutrapelia* (mental diversion)

Eutrapelia (εὐτραπερία) is a Greek word, and it is a virtue listed by Aristotle in *Nicomachean Ethics*. In Japanese it has been translated by both Takada Saburō and Katō Shinrō as *kichi* (*wit*), the mean between the extremes of buffoonery and boorishness. I would suggest that this had been forgotten as a virtue. Even if simply understood as humour or wit, it is a quality that it is far better to possess than not, and if society lightens up a little as a result, then all the better. Note that the etymology of this word means a 'clever shift', referring to the idea of shifting one's mood toward happiness. I feel that in a properly functioning technology-mediated environment, when we are entirely focused on work arrangements that are directed toward accuracy and are governed by restrictive shackles, our self-alienation in relation to machines reaches an extreme, and freedom and creativity fall by the wayside. People need a well-timed disengagement from this situation. As an effective change of pace through hobbies or sport or recreation, *eutrapelia* represents a truly important virtue.

If we think along those lines, then in fact this primarily entails liberating within the arts and imagination our selves that had, as one virtue of self-control, been hemmed in by the constraints of machines and the mechanisms of human organizations. *Eutrapelia* becomes an intellectual virtue that invites others to join us in that space of liberation.

(6) The virtue of temporal ethics

Traditional ethics was a spatial ethics, and there is an ongoing need for this in the future. If someone spatially moves a spatial object by entering my room without authorization and taking my wallet from my drawer without permission and putting it in their pocket, this constitutes the unethical action of theft. Similar questions of temporal ethics, which entail more important consequences, also need to be considered.

As suggested by Millet's painting "The Angelus" (The Evening Bell), in the olden days communities shared a common temporality, with the temple or church bell as their time signal. The diversity of occupations in our urban lives today means that working hours and lifestyles differ from person to person, and time has become the possession of individuals, as symbolized by the fact that everyone owns a watch. Our time, which has become an individual possession, is often at risk of invasion. For instance, inconsiderate sales reps sometimes call up and urge me to buy some shares, purely for their own gain. This interrupts my research and I lose my train of thought, without even having time to jot down what I had been thinking about, and sometimes it is impossible to reconstruct elaborate logic. Such events not only mean that someone has invaded my time without consent and hindered my work, but also that I have been robbed of time. Since my life is the accumulation of my time, being deprived of time means that my life is harmed to that extent. In some cases this might be fatal. This gives rise to a need for the virtue of temporal ethics in various specific forms, such as respecting other people's time. Moral education aimed at preventing new forms of disturbances is also necessary.

In this way, the extraordinary development of information devices has given rise to a whole raft of ethical issues. As noted earlier, one of these is the complete transformation in the concept of neighbour. When needing help in the past we would simply rely, albeit with some hesitation, on our spatial neighbours, but today information devices and the possibility of remote conversations using different types of telephones allow us to contact our family and trusted friends and overcome the crisis effectively. In other words, the increased possibility of mutual support through the expansion of neighbourly relationships via devices in our technology-mediated environment also opens up new dimensions in neighbourly love. If the concept of an unspecified majority of invisible neighbours that transcends face-to-face relations were to take hold, we would realize just how personally urgent an ethical issue is the problem of starvation raised by Peter McCormick. In this way, mechanical devices enable us to provide service to others that was impossible solely through natural means. This leads to the recommendation that we need to acquire the know-how to operate cars and communications devices and other equipment in our technology-mediated society. In the natural world Plato encouraged people to take up *gimnastike* (gymnastics) in order to build up their natural strength, but in our times what is needed is *machinastike*, or the knowledge of how to operate equipment in a technology-mediated environment. This represents a new virtue.

Incidentally, it could be argued that nearly all of the wild fantasies found in fairy tales and folk stories have become reality in the second half of the twentieth century. Human beings have landed on the moon and walked on its surface. Yet what we have simply failed to achieve is a 'shield'. With the advent of the Internet and e-mail, information is sometimes transferred anonymously, and in some cases it is misused.

In addition to such problems, progress in the life sciences has led to many issues pertaining to human dignity being presented via organ transplants and various experiments involving genetic manipulation, such as cloning. *Eco-ethica* must develop an ethics that will act as the basis for carefully debating ideas that are all formulated from perspectives that give free rein to curiosity, such as the possibility of cloning anencephalic babies so as to facilitate organ transplants. To achieve this, interdisciplinary cooperation is necessary on an international scale.

In the realm of nature, form is suggestive of function. Even with man-made goods, in the early days a look at their form would give a general idea of their function. When I was a child, gramophones had a large trumpet, while telephones resembled a human face, with the receiver located in the ear position and the mouthpiece situated where the mouth is on a face. In both instances these devices had little portability. The subsequent evolution of technology succeeded in making all such apparatuses smaller, and devices with different functions all took on the same form—that of a light and compact box. At a glance it is impossible to tell whether a particular device is a cigarette lighter, a miniature camera, a recording device, or a time bomb. Unless people read the attached label and use the device in line with its intended function, the outcome might be fatal. The same goes for all pharmaceuticals. In everyday life in our technology-mediated environment it has become essential to consider the new virtue of safety in all spheres of activity. It is necessary to make a clear ethical distinction between preventive responsibility aimed at ensuring safety and maintenance so that accidents do not occur, and post facto accountability after accidents have unfortunately occurred, and these virtues also need to be clearly formulated.

Important toward that end is the realization that taking responsibility in the form of whistle-blowing is, as a modern version of the classic virtue of courage, an important act aimed at ensuring safety. In the past such people were regarded as inside informants, which gives a negative impression, and in reality this tactic was also used on occasion as a ploy for bringing down one's rivals, through measures such as anonymous letters to newspapers. By contrast, whistle-blowing is a positive act of courage. When people make a dash for the train or there might be something wrong with a carriage, for instance, the conductor and station officials blow a warning whistle in everyone's presence so as to prevent an accident. Hence the term 'whistle-blowing' is preferable in that it better corresponds to a virtue, and I hope that people in each line of work will cooperate to prevent accidents as much as possible and ensure a safe society. Nowadays the term 'accident' is used in the sense of a chance incident, but etymologically this word derives from *accedere*, a Latin verb that means to occur in an ancillary fashion. Although some accidents might indeed have aspects that are not humanly caused, in essence they are all due to human causes, as the inevitable outcome of carelessness and inattentiveness. In that sense, many virtues relating to safety need to be specifically established as morals for people living in our contemporary technology-mediated environment.

Chapter Four

Morals and Logic

THE JAPANESE MORAL CONSCIOUSNESS

If we regard logic as a way of thinking, then how the Japanese think also becomes an issue. Since a way of thinking is primarily a cultural artifact formed within traditional practices, we can expect there to be a logic fashioned by the Japanese culture that has evolved in the island nation of Japan. Our way of thinking is also shaped by language, so we can assume a logic that is characteristic of the Japanese people who live surrounded by the Japanese language. When we consider morals and logic, therefore, one approach is to start out by examining the relationship between the moral consciousness and logic of the Japanese people. We will then move on to consider general human logic in relation to morals.

I have done research on the Japanese moral consciousness based on the classics and the literature on this topic, but here I would like to consider this question based on actual experience. The first time I experienced life as a teacher abroad was for about four years from around 1955. Since then I have been a visiting professor overseas for one year, and nearly every year I travel overseas for an intensive lecture series or an international conference. Recently in particular I have been involved in many committee meetings and lecture series, so I travel abroad about three times a year, spending at least two months a year outside of Japan. Compared with the initial period when I spent time overseas (i.e., the 15 years up until around 1970), the subsequent two decades have witnessed a major shift in how the Japanese are generally regarded. Up until about 1970 Japan's economic power was not very apparent and the Japanese were on the relatively poor side, but they were highly trusted in terms of morality, partly because of the intellectual achievements on the part of many Japanese.

(Atrocities were committed by Japanese during World War II, but these acts were akin to group hysteria in an emergency situation.) Contemporary Japanese have even been regarded as having exemplary manners.

Subsequently, however, the Japanese have had a generally poor reputation in Europe and the United States, as well as in Asia. Perhaps this is attributable to envy at how rapidly Japan conquered the world market. Although Japanese economic power derives in part from the efforts of the Japanese people, an impartial analysis shows that it was also the result of quite self-centred policies—i.e., policies focused on the national interest—on the part of the Japanese government and companies, and that they exploited European and American technology and, ultimately, the neighbouring Asian countries. The poor reputation of Japanese today is perhaps based on justified criticisms, and the boorishness and money-driven attitude of Japanese tourists abroad are no help. This has been attributed to a decline in morals, with tourists acting like nouveaux riches who think that all they need to do is fork out the money and everything will be fine. Indeed I agree that the recent climate in Japan is deplorable, with people thinking only in terms of material gain, not morals.

Nevertheless, I do have some doubts as to whether Japanese morals are in particular decline or a particularly bad state. Few countries have such a low number of fatal incidents and such a well-functioning legal order as Japan. That was certainly the case when this book was first published in the early 1990s. It is normal in Japanese cities for a woman to be able to walk alone at night, something that is impossible in quite a few other countries. Although unfortunate terrorist bombings and shootings by right-wing groups and so on do occur in Japan, sadly these happen everywhere today. In Paris I have experienced at firsthand the horror of a bombing incident in Saint Germain du Pres, and a glance at American newspapers shows that kidnappings are common there. It seems to me that problems—such as moral corruption (notably, checkbook politics), the assassination of key figures, the loosening of sexual mores, and drug abuse—are found everywhere, and in that respect Japan is better off than most places. Or at least it was when I first wrote this book, but that is no longer the case. It seems to me that Japan outstrips other countries in the number of bizarre murders and murders for insurance money, instances of child abuse and infanticide, as well as suicides caused by bullying. In that respect, what is needed is a general awareness that the family is the site of moral education, and we also need to consider venues for such childhood education in the home, as a step toward tackling the social phenomenon of a sudden increase in broken homes (divorces, solo work postings etc.). Restraint on the part of those in the media and techniques for considering how to prevent the abuse of mobile phones and e-mail will also become new ethical issues. In addition, there are cases where technology itself presents and should solve ethical issues.

Consequently, I can no longer support Lafcadio Hearn's assertion that the Japanese have a particularly heightened moral consciousness. In particular, their behaviour overseas and the lack of public morality within Japan show that problems do indeed exist, such as the general commercialism and greed for power, as well as frequent betrayals. To be sure, people outwardly act in a way that will not disturb the legal order, but I believe that the spirit of sacrifice and the spirit of service are not as strong in Japan as elsewhere, so the pluses and minuses balance each other out. Although external order is relatively well maintained in Japan, what sustains order in this densely populated society is the eyes of other people. In terms of the internal issue of what underpins morality, the situation in Japan does not necessarily lend itself to optimism.

When examining Japanese morals from the perspective of *eco-ethica*, we need to consider not just interpersonal relationships, but also relations between people and things, which is one of the issues taken up in *eco-ethica*. So what matters are particularly prominent in Japan in terms of the relationship between people and things? Let me present an anecdotal experience of my own here.

At one time I was officially employed as a professor at a university in Europe, and something dawned on me then. I spent less than a year at the university, but during that time I bought quite a few books. The book collections of the foreign academics were far bigger than my collection had been at their age, but with rare exceptions they were by no means large in relative terms. This does not mean that the European academics didn't read books. They read a great deal at the library or in their offices. And at that time they were far better paid than Japanese academics. Japanese academics usually have so many books that their house is overflowing, but compared with foreign academics they have relatively few books in their university office, and Japanese libraries are poorly stocked.

In my student days I would visit University of Tokyo students or friends at Keio University, and the walls of their rooms would be lined with books. Even today when I visit the homes of good students, I see that they've accumulated so many books that there's almost nowhere to eat or sleep. Student dormitories overseas are so roomy that they will never overflow with books no matter what, but you'd be lucky to find twenty books on the shelves, and they are all neatly arranged.

When business and political figures succeed in Japan, they take up art and antiques. The pieces they acquire are put in storage, rarely to be seen, and nor are they used. Overseas, however, there are outstanding museums, and except for certain massive corporate conglomerates it is rare for such fine works of art to be owned by individuals. This leads to the conclusion that the Japanese have a very strong sense of ownership in relation to things, but little sense of using them. They have piles of unread books (they *own* lots of books), but unfortunately it seems that library usage is very low. This strongly developed sense of ownership rather than usage is also apparent in other situations. For instance, there are places in high-class residential districts in Greater Tokyo where people build a trench around their land and put up a sign saying "No entrance" and don't use the land at all. Or they go and build a parking lot in front of someone's patio. Such acts are indicative of the Japanese illusion that "If you own it, you have the right to use it."

Of course, however, ownership rights do not automatically confer rights of usage. For example, people in Japan are allowed to own a sword, but this does not mean they can promptly go out and brandish it on the streets. It is obvious that ownership rights and usage rights are separate matters, yet in actual life people behave as if they can do whatever they want with their own land or build their house anyhow they like, since they own it. This attitude is disfiguring our cities, and I believe it might also be the cause of problems in the economic and political spheres.

My reflections have led me to conclude that what is needed to bring about a revolution in Japanese consciousness is morality as a standard that transcends the law, morality that arises from within the individual as something distinct from group cohesion, morality in the sense of making cultural events open to the public, and a distinction between ownership and usage.

A related phenomenon is how—unlike in the West, for example—Japanese believe we can rid ourselves of sin and impurities through Shinto prayers and purification ceremonies. Shinto prayers often make mention of how the impurities so removed sink to the bottom of the ocean and are carried off somewhere. Once our impurities and sins are borne away out of sight, one becomes pure. This might be a highly effective perception as a technique for living, but it entails no true repentance. A culture of shame is said to have existed in Japan since olden times, but although this might mean feeling great shame at no longer being able to hold up one's head in public, it does not signify shame at having failed to act ethically. People feel shame vis-à-vis the public. So adapting one's behaviour to meet public standards would not be something of which to be ashamed, even if the public were wrong. This is exactly what going along with public opinion means. In other words, Japan's 'culture of shame' is not an internal 'morality of shame'. In that sense, I believe that Japan does not possess a true culture of shame. It is just that the Japanese are ashamed in relation to others.

Education needs to take these points into consideration when reconstructing Japanese morality. In other words, we must realize that ethical reflection does not consist of listening to the public. Instead, it is a self-referential circular logic.

THE TECHNOLOGY-MEDIATED ENVIRONMENT AND CHANGES IN MORAL CONSCIOUSNESS

Setting aside the particular issue of Japanese morality, I would now like to take up the more general topic of morals and contemporary society. Here the question is just what is meant by contemporary society. The word *society* is bandied about as if its meaning were all too self-evident, but we inevitably envisage society as being based on the environment that we ourselves inhabit as individuals. In my case, for example, I think only of the society revolving around education and research, while for people with links to the corporate world, society would mean the domain they see from their perspective as corporate people. Then there is agricultural society and urban society and so on, so *society* is a highly ambiguous term. In order to clarify what is meant by contemporary society, therefore, we need to understand it on the basis of a particular characteristic.

I believe that contemporary society is characterized by the technology-mediated environment. In my view the term *technology-mediated environment* is synchronously applicable to any society in the world (i.e., it is a phenomenon that is occurring simultaneously around the world).

The history of human civilization can be broadly divided into three periods. The first was when we were using tools. Tools are merely an extension of our limbs and senses. So although their use makes things physically somewhat easier for us, we were still making full use of our own bodies. This period lasted for a long time. Although the nature of the tools used changed over time, we could say that this stage continued right up to the fifteenth or sixteenth century.

Then came the mechanical age. The Japanese word for *machine*, kikai 機械, derives from an old Chinese word that was used in a Taoist work, the *Chuang-Tzu*, while *machina*, from which the English word *machine* is derived, dates back to the days of Greek tragedies, so when defining the word *kikai* a distinction needs to be made between these two senses. But if we think of *kikai* in terms of the literal meaning of the characters—i.e., 'something that has a contraption (*kai* 械) that moves (*ki* 機) by itself'—we can conclude that machines came into existence upon the invention of self-propelling devices with an internal combustion engine—i.e., around the time of the first Industrial Revolution. As readers will be aware, the first steam locomotive was introduced in 1825.

We could also argue that when machines began to interact with each other, the world of a technology-mediated environment came into being for the first time. The invention of the automobile necessitated roads, and electric traffic signals for the smooth regulation of traffic popped up everywhere. The fuel for powering automobiles came to be transported systematically to petroleum complexes, so if any part of the system gets out of kilter, cars won't be able to run.

Nowadays media such as the phone, fax and television enable simultaneous global communications, and various means of transportation also have global networks. The systematic and global formation of such major technology-mediated environments is, I believe, a characteristic of the latter part of the twentieth century. If we look at the world solely in terms of such technology-mediated environments, I think the situation is similar everywhere.

Next I would like to consider the effect of the technology-mediated environment on morality. Let me state upfront that from the perspective of traditional morality, this has very negative aspects. There are also positive aspects that would have been inconceivable in the past and, as outlined in the previous chapter, new virtues are emerging, so we cannot facilely categorize these changes as positive or negative. I would like to examine this question objectively, starting from an analysis of the status quo.

What is readily apparent to any observer is that in a technology-mediated environment skills must be valued above virtues such as love, kindness or sincerity. To take a very simple example, let us look at medical treatment. In the days before tools were invented, the word *treatment* (*te-ate* 手当て in Japanese, which literally means 'laying on of hands') was used to refer to the actual laying of hands on somebody who was exposed to cold winds to protect them from the wind. So in a world without technology 'treating' someone requires real love in some sense. When 'laying hands' on someone, you must at least warm that person up or, if they need cooling down, you have to immerse your hands in cold water and lay them on the person. So 'treatment' was not possible without at least some degree of inner love.

Today, however, treating someone requires skill. In other words, once instruments and machines make their appearance, all that is needed, to put it extremely, is to be highly skilled in using these medical devices. In fact, feeling such pity for the patient that your eyes mist over and you misread the graduation on the needle could actually prove fatal. To put it in extreme terms, skill without kindness is better than kindness without skill.

In other words, we could argue that ultimately a kind of internal erasure is taking place in the realm of the technology-mediated environment. We must give due thought to the fact that we are in a situation where the internal is erased and people are evaluated solely on the basis of their external skills, and where one cannot actually demonstrate kindness or love without outstanding external skills. If matters are left like this, a situation that is highly detrimental to traditional morality will arise. Nevertheless, we are forced to acknowledge that in a technology-mediated environment it is people with outstanding skills who are best able to demonstrate real love. In extreme cases, robots might be more useful than human beings. In car factories, for instance, the use of robots—which have no interiority—has resulted in labour-saving and rescued workers from hard physical labour.

The next characteristic is that human beings are becoming like cogs in a machine. To give an extreme example, school teachers are thought to embody both skills and moral character, but just what is the reality? Suppose an elderly teacher of English as a second language retires. Instead of hiring someone else to take over, the school might, for instance, purchase some equipment that plays recordings of the proper pronunciation, and this device might be used to run pronunciation and conversation classes. Since superb teaching devices that were inconceivable in the past have now appeared, such a scenario is possible. Moreover, *in terms of pronunciation* the English recorded on the equipment in the voice of a native speaker of English would naturally be more correct than the teacher's Japanese-accented English. In that respect we could even argue that the machine is more useful to the students than their teacher. This view maintains that as long as machines can replace human beings in terms of skill, there's nothing wrong with using machines instead of people. To put it extremely, human beings have become cogs in a machine and are used solely for their functionality.

People say that similar situations must have existed even in the past, and it is true that situations capable of changing people did indeed exist in ancient times. Today, however, the idea is that if a highly competent machine is available, it should be used, rather than a human being. Just think of how many machines are used in clinical diagnoses. The unattended operation of machines is also now being viewed through rose-tinted glasses. Following on from the internal erasure mentioned earlier, this shows that personal erasure is also occurring in terms of human functions.

Life today is very convenient. There are even vending machines selling noodles or coffee, so even late at night when you're tired and the stores are closed—or if the shop assistant makes a fuss about having to serve you even if the store is open—you can get whatever you want by inserting some coins and pushing a button. All this seems very handy, but I believe that wordless interaction with mechanical devices basically involves us turning into *things* that associate with other things via codes. This is the second characteristic that appears when contemporary society is characterized as a technology-mediated environment.

The third characteristic is automaton-like reactions as a result of becoming machine 'cogs'. The easiest example to understand is traffic, which was mentioned in the previous chapter. When the signal turns green we have to step off the curb unhesitatingly, and when it changes to red we must stop without hesitation. Since signals demand an accurate and prompt response, they deprive us of the habit of training ourselves to make decisions. The more systems and machines advance, the more pronounced this tendency becomes.

It could be argued that not only does this have a negative impact on our thinking, but it has also created a situation whereby the courtesy of old can no longer be maintained. Let me give a very simple example. In a situation where the traffic light is green and you and your teacher are walking toward each other, even if it's been a decade since you met it would be out of the question to stop in the middle of the road and greet each other. Whether the other person is your teacher or a work colleague, you have to pass on by with at best a "Hello". If you want to be truly polite, you could retrace your steps in the direction the teacher is heading, but do you really have time for that? In such chance encounters on the road, we yield authority to the traffic signal, rather than to human courtesy. This is a very simple example, but I could cite many others. This tendency is even more pronounced in automobile societies. If you look in the rear vision mirror and notice your teacher in the car behind you, you can't just politely wave him ahead of you. There is no choice but to abide by the physical order. To put it bluntly, "first in, first served". For better or for worse, that's how things stand these days.

The fourth characteristic is even more deplorable. Even when others have to be treated as cogs in a machine, as described above, or where we ourselves must behave in that manner, we are far from being machines—we are indeed alive. Nevertheless, responding directly to stimuli means that we are no longer human and that we are no different from other living creatures. Animals in the wild live in response to signals, but human beings rejected the behaviorist responses found in nature and created another realm (that of the technology-mediated environment), out of a desire to fashion a higher-order world. Yet a look at how people behave in this world of the technology-mediated environment shows that in most cases we respond animalistically, just as animals respond to natural phenomena.

So in that case human beings might be defined as animals living in the new world of the technology-mediated environment, but how appropriate would that be? It is a well-known fact that animals of the same species always greet each other, except when facing extreme danger. Even ants do this, and dogs likewise go through the motions of greeting each other. Yet human beings (at least those in urban societies) don't even do that.

When you go out for lunch, some people will ask "Is this seat taken?" before pulling up a chair at an occupied table (unless it's someone from the same company), but it is extremely unfortunate that most people just plump themselves down without so much as a by-your-leave, and they don't say a word even if the waiter brings an appetizing-looking dish for the other person or if that person seems to be really enjoying the food. In fact, engaging in conversation makes people think there's something odd about you or that you're a nuisance. In societies that are still somewhat easy-going, there are cities where it is conventional to at least say something like "Bon appétit". In nearly all major cities, however, if the other person is a total stranger then people eat their meal without even making eye contact—even if sitting opposite each other—as if the other person were a piece of wood. If words are exchanged, it does not go beyond asking permission to read the sports newspaper the other person put down when the meal arrived. You don't even say goodbye when the person gets up to leave. Such behaviour might seem deserving of criticism, but when you think about it, we rub shoulders with crowds of people of our species every day on the trains, and were we to greet each and every one we would soon lose our voice, and we'd also get a crick in the neck from nodding to people.

Circumstances today, then, have forced us to abandon the habit of greeting each other. Up in the mountains even aloof people will say hello, and if Japanese come across a compatriot in a lonely desert or in a country village in a place like Poland or Bulgaria where they don't speak the local language at all, they will indeed smile, as if greeting an animal of the same species, and they will at least ask where the other person comes from. Yet in societies where English or French is spoken, Japanese rarely say hello when they run into each other. And if foreigners are in a car together, they don't converse (unless they have some particular reason for doing so). This means that unless people really need to ask for directions, or in special circumstances such as when filled with an unusual sense of liberation on vacation, in urban life people's behaviour does not usually even reach the level of animals. So we could say that although humans are indeed living, flesh-and-blood beings, they have become like machine cogs.

The upshot is that ethics in such societies resembles physical adjustments among physical objects. For instance, during rush hour in Tokyo there are people whose job it is to cram as many commuters as possible onto the trains, and even very standoffish people push to get aboard. This is just like trying to cram as much as possible into a suitcase. If you fail to bend your body in such a situation, those around you might think you are inconsiderate or lacking in morals. Ultimately, this could be described as a physical adjustment whereby you move in an effective direction in accordance with the numbers.

It seems to me that when human self-alienation in the form of objectification thus becomes a reality in our daily lives, such as in commuting—commuting by car is similar in that it is an extension of the above-mentioned automatic blind obedience to signals—we are no longer living in a free world, but merely moving in the dimension of arbitrariness and necessity.

The logic of dehumanization extends to everyday economic actions such as purchases. Nowadays we use a vast range of vending machines to obtain stamps and various other goods. As long as we insert the correct coins and push the right button, we can obtain what we want through the routine operation of the machine. So even when we get what we want, there is no need for gratitude, as it's only to be expected. According to statistics, there were about six million vending machines throughout Japan in 1988, so if we assume that the population at that time was 120 million, this would mean one vending machine for every 20 or so people. Since more and more of these machines are being produced every day, nowadays the figure might be closer to one for every 18 people. That would mean there are more vending machines around town than trees. That's the kind of environment we're living in today. In this environment acquiring goods is understood as a phenomenon of inevitably dehumanized relationships, and gratitude is nonexistent. From that perspective, all that is needed as far as the things of this world are concerned is the economy and machines. No human emotions whatsoever are required, so ethics degenerates into human engineering.

I believe that the five characteristics above are issues of logic as a way of thinking that is related to morality and that is readily comprehensible in our world of a technology-mediated environment. I am not saying this is good or bad. I am simply saying that we need to consider such issues then think about reconstructing morality.

THE LOGICAL STRUCTURE OF ACTION

So let's now consider whether any new moral issues have arisen as far as formal logic is concerned, rather than logic as a way of thinking or frame of mind.

Why is formal logic being discussed in a work on ethics? The answer is that the areas in which our ethics are called into question relate mainly to actions, and actions derive from people's thinking, so it is only natural that we would examine formal logic, which is a manifestation of the threads of people's thought.

So what kind of logical structure do people experience when they undertake a certain action? The reasoning put forward by Aristotle in *Nicomachean Ethics* represents a classic view on this question. Nicomachus was Aristotle's son, and he compiled Aristotle's lectures into a book manuscript. According to *Nicomachean Ethics*, people start out with the belief that a certain something is desirable, and since they want this, it is formulated as a purpose. They then search for means that will enable the realization of that purpose. In this way, when considering how to achieve our purpose, we think of various means toward that end at virtually the same time, even though we don't always list them down on paper. So if we want money, we think about different ways of obtaining it, such as selling off our possessions, borrowing from the bank or a friend, taking on part-time work, or stealing. Aristotle advocated choosing the most noble (*kallista*) and most expedient (*rhasta*) means from among the many different possibilities. If on the basis of the major premise of wanting money it turns out that borrowing from a friend, for instance, is the most expedient approach and the amount is something we can repay, we decide to borrow the money. So we visit our friend to ask for a loan. Out of the various possible means $p, q, r \ldots$, therefore, we move from the means r toward our purpose A.

Here the purpose is self-evident. Our desire for money is obvious to us. For doctors, there is the major premise of wanting to cure a particular patient, so the doctor considers what needs to be done to achieve that. The treatment will be decided on after the doctor considers whether to advise a change of air, an operation, medication, or all of these concurrently, or whether to refer the patient to another doctor. This is all very obvious, but it is such matters that constitute the logical structure of action.

Let's look at it another way. Suppose you have the religious ideal of becoming one with God, and you think about how to achieve this desire. Various possibilities spring to mind—entering a monastery, going to a temple, donating property to the poor, working as a volunteer, buying and reading the Bible, taking lessons from a priest or minister, taking up the study of Zen, and so on. Your job prevents you from retiring to a temple or monastery, so you decide on the means of doing volunteer work just on Sundays. These moves toward your goal constitute action. When people are deciding on a course of action, they follow this kind of logic.

This was known as the logical structure of action, and nobody had come up with any more recent ideas, but from early on I had wondered whether this alone was adequate as the logical structure of action in our new world of a technology-mediated environment. For the past decade I have acted as the chair of an international research council on new ethics, and one distant reason for this was that I had formulated a logic of action different from that proposed by Aristotle. When you hear it you might think "That's it?", but formulating this logically is no easy matter.

In short, it is not that the purpose is self-evidently desired; it is that a powerful means P is self-evidently available in society. Electricity and nuclear power are instances of this. Albeit in a different form, large capital is another example. At that self-evident point the question arises of what purposes can be achieved by using the force P as a powerful means. So the means P is self-evident, and what is then set out as possibilities are those things that are analytically conceivable given that particular means P and whose materialization is thought to be inevitably feasible. These are listed as purposes, and from amongst these one purpose must be selected on the basis of some principle.

When once asked about what to choose ethically, Aristotle advocated choosing the means that is the most expedient and also the noblest. Even today, when power constitutes the underlying premise, we must strive to choose the best purpose out of all the possibilities that can be achieved through power. In terms of the actual form this takes, we decide which of the achievable various purposes is the most convenient and the most economically effective. Economic effectiveness is indeed one criterion on which companies must of course rely when making their decisions, but whether that is the logically best course of action should also be kept in mind. Since Aristotle's logic contained the two conditions of "most expedient" and "noblest", I think it is acceptable to substitute "economically effective" for "expedient" in the logic I have presented, but we must retain "noblest".

Admittedly, in the logical structure of contemporary action presented here there is a reversal of the structure in logical terms, in the sense that the means becomes the major premise and the purposes become the minor premises. People became aware of this reversal when I gave my presentation in 1955. This has been commented on—for instance, in the French philosopher Paul Ricoeur's *Philosophy*—as a contribution to Japanese philosophy in the form of the discovery of a new ethical structure.

Not only is there an overall reversal of these two logical structures, but there are other major differences as well. Aristotle's classical thinking still applies today at the level of the individual. We can also, however, entertain hopes that are other-worldly—i.e., that are removed from this world—such as how to become one with God, as in the example mentioned above. The logical structure that operates at the level of the individual has the limitation that today, when the means are massive physical forces, only physical phenomena made possible by these forces can emerge as purposes.

Again, under the classic Aristotelean formula the individual makes the decisions, but with the modern formula that I have proposed a committee makes the decisions, or the government makes the decisions, or the military makes the decisions, or a company makes the decisions. In this way, the agent of decision is the group. In actual political and corporate actions, the agent consists of an entity such as a committee that bears a kind of collective responsibility. Since such entities partake in actions, it is important to give thought to these matters so that the locus of moral responsibility in such cases is a little clearer. This is a completely new issue that has emerged as a result of the pluralization of the ethical subject. In the past ethics and morality were internal issues for the individual, but nowadays group ethics or group morality needs to be considered—although this does not mean it should take a form that ignores individuals.

Today committee ethics are being handled in the realm of individual ethics. Suppose a decision made by a committee has a bad outcome. Responsibility currently seems to be dealt with overtly through the resignation of the chair or committee members. The outcome is that they have taken responsibility legally, but not morally. We need to acknowledge that taking responsibility merely means that an individual who is moral feels moral anguish; actual ethical or moral responsibility is not being considered in a form whereby the logical structure is reversed.

From that perspective, we are living in an age when we are facing issues of truly momentous proportions. At a time when potency far exceeding that unleashed by the single atomic bomb that destroyed a whole city in 1945 is anticipated, a powerful means P is available, and we have to select a purpose from amongst several possible scenarios whereby P is put to use. In such a time we need to reflect on just how moral is our thinking. Even if it is not a matter of choosing the means, but instead the purpose, this still constitutes an action, so it is essential for us as human beings to take the moral aspects of this action into account.

In the past 'loyalty' spread from loyalty to a minor lord to loyalty to an entire nation and, among young people today, to loyalty on an international scale. Similarly, if everyone becomes aware of such matters, then when seeking out certain purposes inherent in a particular force we must consider not which purpose is advantageous, but which is noble.

The two practical syllogisms described so far can be illustrated schematically as follows:

TECHNOLOGICAL ABSTRACTION— A NEW FORM OF ABSTRACTION

There are many ramifications of the foregone fact that massive power deriving from science and technology is available to us in various forms as self-evident means. One of the most notable outcomes is the saving of time and labour. A clear example is lifts and elevators. Simply pressing a button takes us up to the 48th floor in a minute without walking or tiring at all, even if we have heavy things to carry. Suppose you were to walk up to the 48th floor

Table 4.1: Logical structures (syllogisms) of action

	Aristotle (classical formula)	Imamichi (contemporary formula)
Major premise	Formulation of a goal: I want A.	Verification of the means: P is available.
Minor premise	Selection of means: 1) $p, q, r, s, t \ldots$ will *probably* enable the desired outcome A. 2) Out of the possibilities listed, which is the most expedient and noblest?	Selection of purpose: 1) $a, b, c, d \ldots$ are potential outcomes of the P in our possession. 2) Out of the possibilities listed, which is the most effective?
Conclusion	Action: $p \rightarrow A$	Action: $P \rightarrow a$

carrying lots of heavy books. At my age this would be well nigh impossible. Modern civilization is achieving marvels through science and technology. This involves minimizing the processes as much as possible in order to obtain maximum results. I will refer to this as technological abstraction.

I believe this is a new form of logical abstraction, but to avoid confusion I will refer to it as technological abstraction. Conventional abstraction involves the mental operation of factoring out specific representations of individual beings (i.e., excluding them from one's consciousness) and abstracting (i.e., extracting and focusing on) their common attributes to formulate a concept. By contrast, technological abstraction could be described as factoring out the processes and abstracting the outcome. This has numerous convenient and welcome aspects.

One of the ethically important aspects is the ability to reduce the handicaps faced by people who are physically challenged. With a cable car, even those incapable of climbing mountains can enjoy the view from the summit in twenty to thirty minutes. On the other hand, there is no denying that the practice of climbing mountains on foot has largely disappeared, and the training in virtues—such as friendship in the form of helping each other, perseverance, austerity, and courage—that was coincidentally fostered in the process is on the decline.

Notwithstanding this, labour-saving has transformed housework. Not only does the labour-saving resulting from the use of household appliances during cooking, cleaning and washing make it easy for women to move into society, but mechanization has also enabled them to move into workplaces that were previously restricted to men with their superior physical strength—e.g., the military and the police—and so this has awakened society to equal rights for men and women.

In these ways technological abstraction has brought about changes that are of great interest from an ethical perspective, but this abstraction is also an ethical innovation from the viewpoint of transforming how we think. Of particular importance here is the fact that technological abstraction eliminates processes (i.e., temporality). Yet since awareness as the essence of human existence is not spatial in the first place, but temporal, the fact that technological abstraction compresses temporality means that it compresses the human essence in the direction of nihilization. We simply cannot afford to overlook this reality. Adapting to and living in a technological society has meant following the path of dehumanization, compounding the existing trend toward being alienated by material objects.

In order to reinstate ethics, therefore, we must freely restore time as process. Aesthetic experiences through the arts have no meaning if their temporality is lost, so they would be helpful in this restoration of ethics, and in that sense the involvement of aesthetics in ethics is vital.

SELF-REGULATION OF TECHNOLOGY AND OF HUMANS

No-one would argue with the proposition that technology has made our lives easier in many ways—that it is bringing about social good by improving people's lives. But suppose we expand the timescale of social morality and consider historical or future morality. If, for example, science and technology continue to evolve in the same fashion as they have to date, then we are forced to question whether this is acceptable as far as the human race in a hundred years' time is concerned, given the existence of issues such as how to deal with all the rubbish or with unavoidable nuclear power accidents (for instance, the walls of nuclear reactors are part of the physical world, so they are gradually eroding, and failure might occur someday even if maintenance is carried out meticulously).

We could also expand the spatial scale of social morality and consider morality in terms of the universe. Perhaps this could be included in future morality, but what I am referring to here is morality in relation to our current atmosphere. For instance, it is said that if we continue to use chlorofluorocarbons in various devices or to make our lives more convenient, the ozone layer will be depleted, life systems on earth will be harmed, and people will die miserable deaths from ailments such as skin cancer. Other atmospheric emissions will lead to such consequences as acid rain, the death of evergreen trees, and dramatic changes in global conditions as a result of climate change. We are forced to conclude that as long as science and technology are not self-regulated, the human race is hastening the destruction of all nature.

Hence the self-regulation of science and technology is essential for the survival of the human race, and this must firstly be considered in terms of historical morality and morality toward our universe. If, however, this led to ethics being regarded as social engineering for the sake of human survival, it would end up as such a technologically oriented way of thinking that it would be transformed into technology aimed only at actual effects, even in a field such as ethics that seeks the values of goodness and beauty. Rather than mere survival, what is important above all is surviving with dignity—i.e., living *well*.

So we need to realize that the self-regulation of science and technology must be considered not only from the viewpoint of science and technology, but also as the self-regulation of human beings. In other words, this self-regulation should not consist of feedback on science and technology, but human self-regulation. This demands opportunities where those who are truly thinking about ethics—not just scientists, politicians and economists—can become involved in large numbers and consider these issues collectively.

For the sake of brevity, I will refer here to science and technology simply as technology. While retaining its attributes as a tool, technology has taken on the form of machines and created a whole environment. As we have seen, however, it has brought about a revolution in people's attitudes and is encroaching within people, while also retaining its attributes as their environment. Through five turning points, this has already transformed logic as a fundamental way of thinking and reversed the syllogism of action, and it has now reached the stage of presenting human self-regulation in the form of the self-regulation of technology.

In a nutshell, this progress in technology could be described as technology gradually changing from an external force to something that constitutes the environment and surroundings in which we live and then infiltrating within us. Transcending even the inconceivable (i.e., an internal correspondence between technology and human beings), technology is becoming an internal structure within us. When we think about high-performance computers and large computers that think on behalf of people, it is patently obvious that technology is being internalized within human beings.

One major issue that this poses right now is therapeutic ethics, which is linked to medicine. As readers will be aware, science has encroached on the human body. For instance, technology has improved to the point where patients can be treated with organ transplants from other people. Yet this raises a host of issues. Remember that Kant argued that human beings are an end in themselves and should never be regarded as a means. Bodily organs are not human beings, so it is acceptable to make use of them, but we should remember that their owner is a human being. Proponents of organ transplants argue that if brain death is accepted as the end of life, transplants can save the lives of patients suffering from incurable diseases. Yet brain death in turn raises another issue—i.e., the possibility of a reversal in a condition identified as brain death. In other words, there is the question of whether a state of temporary brain death might exist, as well as concern that this might not constitute actual death. Be that as it may, anyone familiar with human beings must take into account the fact that even if it were possible to determine definitively that brain death does constitute actual death, there is the possibility of crimes involving false pronouncements of brain death.

In reality, we already hear about people purchasing kidneys from poor youths in developing countries, and there have been cases of these people being taken to a developed country on the promise that they'll be given help in finding work. Under the pretext of a blood test, they are injected with an anaesthetic, and while they are asleep a kidney is removed and then used for transplant surgery. Some parents with a sick child have also requested that instead of aborting their next child its kidney be removed immediately after birth so as to save a sick older sibling, and that the newborn then be allowed to die. If such actions bring greater evil into the world and we have no way of knowing what criminal attempts might be made by people with money and power under the pretext of saving lives, then we need to think about protecting the dignity of human beings before protecting the dignity of life. I want to be of as much use to others as possible as long as I draw breath, and if I can be of use even after death, I would like to do so. Yet if that promotes egoism and evil in others, then I must refrain from any involvement.

In the autumn of 1990 the pioneers of organ transplants, Joseph Murray and E. Donnall Thomas, won a Nobel Prize, so no doubt we will see further developments in this direction. Nevertheless, it is my view that if the goal lies strictly in curing human disease, then rather than depriving others of their body parts we should move toward developing artificial organs through rivalry among the life sciences, medicine and biotechnology, so as to cure people by providing them with artificial organs. I support this because it is in the direction of living—and allowing to live—without depriving others of their life force. This could be regarded as advice from the field of *eco-ethica* to the field of medicine, as well as a directive that human nature issues in relation to human capabilities.

Responsibility for the current measures to prolong life at all cost without questioning the meaning of life must be laid largely at the feet of us philosophers and ethicists, but it is regrettable that the general public is forgetting this.

Chapter 4

THE MYTHOS OF FIRE

Let me take this opportunity to discuss the question of nuclear power and ethics. Laypeople like myself who have no special knowledge of nuclear power want to ask those in the field what on earth are they thinking.

When we consider our usage of electricity and hear that nuclear power provides nearly thirty percent of Japan's power supply and is expected to account for as much as fifty or sixty percent in the twenty-first century, even people with absolutely no expertise in this field realize that nuclear energy is indispensable as a source of everyday energy and that it must be used. The following discussion might seem far removed from such concerns, but I would like us to pause and consider the mythos—i.e., myth—of fire.

Whenever fire has been given to humans, tragedy has always occurred. In the Edo period (1603–1867), a peaceful era with few wars, four things were cited as the most fearful—i.e., earthquakes, lightning, fire and father. Fathers are to be feared because in anger they breathe fire. So everything that arouses fear in people has a connection with fire. Fire is the origin of all things fearful. So what happened when this fearful fire made its appearance?

In Greek mythology the god Prometheus, who was concerned over the future of mortals, stole fire from the palace of Zeus, the Lord of the Gods, and gave it to mortals. This allowed human civilization to make great advances, but Prometheus was severely punished, being left naked on a mountaintop for an eagle to pick at his liver while he was still alive. This is the tragedy of a hero-god, because the abuse of fire also exacerbated the disasters befalling the human race.

How does Japanese mythology portray the appearance of fire? The deities Izanagi and Izanami entered into sexual union and gave birth to various gods. When giving birth to Kagutsuchi, the god of fire, Izanami burned her genitals, and this caused her death. In other words, because these two major gods gave birth to the god of fire in the same way as with the other gods of nature, taking no special precautions at all, the goddess ended up dying from her burns. Fire was the symbol of human beings, as distinct from animals. Whenever it appears, the person who caused the fire is always punished or dies.

Nuclear power is an energy source that generates massive amounts of electricity, but it is an awe-inspiring fire. We must not forget that according to old ideas of morality, those who handle such a fire will be punished. Prometheus simply gave people fire in accordance with the old ideas. People had not yet thought about a new morality or a new way of life as a result of receiving fire, so the gods' punishment consisted of punishing the one who gave them fire so precipitously. The same applied to the Japanese god of fire, Kagutsuchi.

Hence I truly believe that unless we change our thinking completely, we must abandon the use of nuclear energy. What would a completely new way of looking at things consist of? Giving priority to profits and gain when starting up an enterprise is nothing new, as this idea has been around for thousands of years. Using your power to protect your country and attack your enemies is another way of thinking that has been around for thousands of years. I believe that we should use nuclear power only when we can abandon such ways of thinking.

In other words, unless we become far more moral than in the past, we should not use nuclear energy. I know nothing about nuclear power, but given human fallibility, how can scientists boast that a particular piece of equipment is absolutely safe? It is crucial to think twice—thrice—as to what steps should be taken if the equipment breaks down. Unless disaster science and disaster management are studied more fully and perfected, this terrifying fire must not be put into use.

To make matters worse, most people working with nuclear power have never studied ethics. Is this acceptable? Better late than never. It might be mere theory, but unless these people who have not even studied the old morality study ethics, unless they seek out a new morality, surely it is unacceptable for them to wield the power of technology merely on the basis of commonsense, legislation, engineering knowledge and corporate strategies? Why is it that the Japanese government downplays philosophy and ethics even in the senior high school curriculum?

The body of knowledge known as ethics is encapsulated in works written by scholars with a passion for ethics. I question whether it is acceptable for people who have never read a single one of these books to work in the field of nuclear energy. I don't care if I upset those who are working in this field to the best of their ability. I don't care if they tell me I'm talking a load of rubbish. No matter what people might say, I will continue to speak out—humbly, with cap in hand—urging them to devote full attention to even a single book on ethics. The present book, for instance, might be insignificant, but it embodies the philosophical pursuits of our forebears—i.e., the traditions of ethics—as well as my own hard-won philosophical thinking on an *eco-ethica* for the future.

Admittedly, I have no knowledge of nuclear energy from a research or business perspective. Nevertheless, I would dispute the tenets that are advocated in Japan as the three principles of nuclear energy and which appear in Article 2 of the Atomic Energy Basic Law. This law sets forth democratic management, independent performance, and publicizing of the results as the three principles for peaceful uses of atomic energy.

But surely the most important points are the "peaceful purposes" and "safety" mentioned in the law? I would argue categorically that nuclear energy must be used only in peace industries. Anything else is unacceptable. And surely "ensuring safety" is an equally important principle? I think only two principles are necessary in relation to nuclear energy. Democratic management, independent performance and publicizing the results are all operational matters, not fundamental principles. What is of supreme importance are the two ethical principles of "ensuring safety" and limiting the use of nuclear energy to "peaceful purposes". I would argue that these are issues of morality in our new age and that they lead to the study of *eco-ethica*. There are various other more ethical matters relating to this, but here I will focus briefly on the important themes.

The following comments will sound harsh to those who are working tirelessly in the field of nuclear energy and taking their research seriously, but there has been a spate of accidents at nuclear power facilities. Although those in the industry say accidents are very rare, the operational nature and number of nuclear facilities mean that there is the possibility of a major accident, and even minor accidents cause lasting damage to the surrounding areas. Moreover, most of these accidents are not the result of natural disasters but of human error or equipment malfunction. It is immoral to forget that human beings are accident-prone, imperfect and self-vindicating and to even think about profits when we are still not adequately prepared. The things of this world are destined to perish. There are no walls that are permanently indestructible, so it is immoral to make people believe such things, because nuclear reactor accidents make many in the surrounding regions sick for generations to come.

Given the present state of physics, engineering and technology, therefore, the nuclear power industry has no rightful qualifications to operate on a commercial basis, and for now this work should be undertaken by an international federation of countries or an alliance of churches, operating on a non-profit basis that takes safety into consideration. Premature though the current situation might be, however, the clock cannot be turned back on how existing companies operating on the competitive principle of profit-making have started up this industry, and on how 'modern fire' fraught with a dangerous new mythos (myth) is being commercialized as an energy source on a scale that extends beyond our planet.

In that case, researchers, business leaders and workers involved with nuclear energy must take up a revolution in moral consciousness as their own challenge and, in a dialogue with philosophers, seek out an ideology different from that of existing companies and ideals at variance with the existing corporate mentality. Admittedly, a corporate ethics that does not simply pursue profits but has also made massive donations has also been in existence. So why not establish a major institution for carrying out research into safety issues and this new ethics? It seems to me that people involved with nuclear energy are proud of their work and believe they shoulder the destiny of their times, and they get so carried away that they end up in a world of their own. The same goes for those in the fields of biotechnology and medicine.

I don't mind if my comments anger them. Both sides need to speak what's on their mind. The days are gone when it was enough to consider the fate of humanity in terms of the next few generations. We are now in a time when it is necessary to think about humankind's fate for hundreds and thousands of years ahead and to give serious consideration to the likelihood of human survival. It would be premature to conclude that the fire of nuclear power is the sole form of energy that can link nature and technology and to gamble everything on that alone.

Even if nuclear power were the only such means, at most its potential uses consist solely of generating electricity—i.e., power for work in this world. To put a negative spin on this, nuclear power is useful only for destroying the things of this world and despoiling life on earth. So we need to reflect on what should be done so that this extreme form of power can be used for more noble purposes. Even if self-denial is impossible for human beings, we must abandon the logic of force whereby human arbitrariness is permitted unconditionally. It is precisely when they have power that human beings, who have the nostalgia of a self-referential turning point, must seek out a contemplative ethics that considers such matters in depth.

I am a layman when it comes to nuclear energy, but here I have spoken about this mythos of fire with a fiery passion. My remarks about those in the nuclear energy industry also apply, I believe, to technology as a whole. Technology has used nature to help human beings, but it has also devastated nature and reduced us to unthinking creatures. We're at a point where it is absolutely critical to change people's attitudes toward nature.

Chapter Five

Human Beings and Nature

THE POSITION OF HUMAN BEINGS IN PRIMORDIAL NATURE

Talk of human beings and nature leads to the initial assumption that since we live in nature this will involve a discussion about human beings as a life form and their surrounding world—i.e., human beings and their environment. It is indeed vital to consider this issue from that perspective, and it is certainly possible to substitute the question of human beings and their environment for that of human beings and nature. I would like to preface my remarks here with something striking that relates directly to this issue.

The Meiji-period novelist Roka Tokutomi (born as Kenjirō Tokutomi) is not read much nowadays, but his name still lingers in places such as Roka Park. He was the younger brother of the journalist and historian Iichirō Tokutomi, who was a highly active nationalist during World War II. Unlike his older brother, Roka was a writer who felt things deeply. His book *Shizen to jinsei* (Nature and Man), which appeared on 15 August 1900, clearly regards nature as constituting one environment for human beings. The book contains passages that inevitably arouse deep emotion when read today, so I would like to present one of these here.

The title of this short piece is "Country Smoke". Let me quote the opening passage:

> I love smoke. I love the smoke of rural houses. My heart is gladdened when I gaze down on wreaths of smoke beckoning back and forth between distant villages and nearby hamlets and wafting leisurely to the sky.

This was written in the Meiji period, so the description of smoke should be recited sonorously. Today virtually nobody would say something like "I love smoke", unless "smoke" was replaced with "cigarettes". Nowadays smoke is regarded as a form of pollution, so enjoying smoke as part of the scenery is a thing of the past. In all likelihood the smoke in this piece was from preparations for the evening meal. Pale blue smoke is probably drifting upward from a row of straw roofs. Gazing down on such a scene from a hill as dusk stole quietly in would have evoked images of a quiet and peaceful life.

When we think about this—when we consider nature as our environment and discuss the relationship between human beings and nature—we cannot help but feel keenly the enormous changes being triggered in our surroundings by the currents of the times. Nowadays nobody would write a piece that started out with "I love smoke", and no-one would enjoy watching smoke drift skyward. In reality, it is smoke that is causing the sights I see as my plane approaches Japan or when I pass Mt Fuji on the Bullet Train. Although it might be a sign of the manufacturing on which Japanese industry is built, even I, a layman when it comes to medical matters, am forced to wonder whether it is acceptable how smoke is blighting the landscape and polluting the atmosphere. In short, this topic falls within the ambit of *eco-ethica*.

So first we will examine the question of human beings and nature along the lines considered by Roka Tokutomi, for now regarding our environment as consisting of nature, and then we will consider human beings' position within this. Even at this point, however, it must be acknowledged that the old ideas differ in their very point of departure from those of today. Almost up until the 1930s people's lives were largely in harmony with nature, both in the East and the West. Certainly, throughout recorded history the relationship between human beings and nature has evolved in a form that asserts human dominance over nature. Even so, it would be reasonable to conclude that human beings have adopted the approach of living in harmony with nature. This is symbolized by the difference between wooden or thatched houses and concrete.

Except for primitive humans, ever since the dawn of history we have made use of nature and regarded ourselves as being at its centre. So when the relationship between human beings and nature is considered primarily in terms of the natural environment, human beings are regarded as being positioned at the centre. In three-dimensional terms, we occupy a position at the centre and also dominate nature—a position akin to that of ruler in nature, because no other living creatures seem to have been so intent on conquering and exploiting nature.

So in a certain sense, we are indeed suffocating nature as our environment, or sucking resources from nature and exploiting them. Yet as the Tokutomi passage illustrates, nature and human beings have been able to coexist in harmony to some extent. The smoke seen drifting upwards was the result of someone starting a fire using materials found in and taken from nature, such as firewood or coal. Then using natural water, they boiled rice and barley taken from nature. The saucepan was also probably made from natural materials. Aluminium did exist in those days, I believe, but in the countryside they would have used earthen pots. It is important to note that this smoke enhanced the natural landscape. No matter how much man-made technology might have been involved, there was a certain sense of unity with nature.

Another important fact is that human beings are aware of occupying the dominant position in nature. It is essential, however, to consider their position in ancient times. In myths—for instance, the Japanese myths that appear in the *Kojiki* and *Nihon Shoki*—the gods are usually portrayed anthropomorphologically. Even the intercourse between the gods Izanagi and Izanami is described as if they were people. The images of the gods created by Greek sculptors such as Phidias and Praxiteles—for example, the image of the goddess Athena—are presented in the form of human beings, so when we think of gods we imagine them as being based on ourselves. Perhaps this is only natural.

Yet in Japanese mythology a golden kite helped Emperor Jimmu to victory, and then a bird called the Yata crow appeared and the emperor followed after it. We must give due thought to the fact that a bird, not a person, led the way. In the past people could not fly, no matter how much they might have wished they could, so at one time birds, which could wheel freely through the sky, were regarded as superior to humans. And just think how things must have been even further back in time, beyond the myths.

I'm sure some readers will have seen photos of Stone Age works of art in art anthologies—i.e., the rock paintings drawn at Lascaux and Altamira in prehistoric times. Actually, these are cave paintings, rather than rock paintings. I would urge readers to take a look at such photos one day. These cave paintings are the oldest extant figurative work produced by human beings. And all they show is animals. None depict people.

What does this signify? The paintings at Lascaux and Altamira were not drawn just anywhere in the caves, but deep inside where the sun does not reach and where they are not readily visible. Another striking fact is that several paintings were painted over the top of the original painting, which means that these were not drawn for purposes of aesthetic appreciation. You might think that people could just use a torch to look at them, but you can't have a torch burning inside a hole for long, so the fact that these paintings are found in such dark places shows that they were not necessarily drawn to be looked at. In 1962 the Deutsches Museum in Munich displayed a replica of the Altamira cave. There are countless overlapping paintings of the same animal, but people are nowhere to be seen. Searching carefully for any other characteristic feature, I found various scratches on the animal paintings. Scholars have put forward various theories as to their origin, but let me outline the hypothesis proposed by Siegfried Giedion. He is a scholar who has also worked in the field of architecture, and his theory that these paintings were used as magic is currently the most persuasive. According to Giedion's hypothesis, these paintings were produced for hunting purposes. If someone intended to go out hunting the next day, he would draw a picture of the animal he wanted to hunt—e.g., a bison or deer—and then scratch it with the tip of an arrow or his spear. So these paintings were not actually intended as art. Instead a hunter would perform a magical rite and pray for success in the hunt next day, and after drawing a painting he would scratch it with an arrow, instead of actually shooting off the arrow. This represented a kind of self-suggestion. So why did they do this? In those days people had no effective tools and nowhere near enough confidence to pride themselves as rulers on earth. When an animal passed by, all they could do was creep up behind it in a large group and shoot it. Or they could take the cowardly path of patiently awaiting an opportunity with bated breath, and when an animal passed by they would suddenly yell out and chase it toward a secret trap they had set. The cave paintings were a mental weapon preparing them for this.

One might argue that human beings were quite intellectually superior by the time they were able to draw paintings, but history up to then shows that they were simply creatures who could do no more than wait with bated breath until a wild animal had passed proudly by and then attack from behind in a large group, since they could not fight as individuals. For anyone who knows shame, this was a shameful position. And the following fact shows that human beings knew such shame. As noted earlier, there are no paintings of people. Any pictures of people that do exist always show them wearing a mask of a bird or a beast. So people's limbs and bodies are visible in these prehistoric cave paintings, but not their faces. The face was related to pride and shame. People were so abject that they thought their own face was not worth leaving behind somewhere. Or perhaps they did not show their face because they were ashamed of this. So the further back we go in time, the less likely are the gods to be depicted in human form. It is important to realize that the ancient gods all took the form of animals.

Just as all the masks in cave paintings depicted birds or animals, in primitive times birds and animals were gods, both in the East and the West. As a look at Egyptian sculptures shows, there too we find gods with the body of a person and just the face of a lion or bird. In China it is always the dragon that is depicted as the creature closest to heaven. This is probably because in long-ago days the awe and fear of large monsters was passed from mouth to mouth, and this transmogrified into a dragon. Likewise in old Japanese myths, where the hydra known as Yamata no Orochi demanded human sacrifices and was regarded as more powerful than humans. Both in the East and West, the strong were represented as animals.

What this means is that we were not from the outset the ruler of our natural environment. We had to rely on gods in order to overcome our fears and avoid unhappiness. The gods are supernatural entities possessing powers to which ordinary beings can never aspire. A supernatural entity could be defined as a being that will aid those trembling in fear, so it must be enormously powerful. What was used to represent such beings figuratively was not the faces of human beings, but those of birds and beasts. When human beings gaze up at the sky from the valleys and see an eagle cutting its way even through storms, they yearn to fly like a bird. They might wish they could swim across the seas or a river, but there is no way they could do so against swift currents. So if they see a snake or fish swimming off as if it owns the waters, it is only natural to regard it as stronger than humans. Even a single beast or bird revered in that way had the power to kill several or dozens of people.

So we must clearly recognize that what we now scorn as dumb animals were once regarded as the symbol of supernatural beings that transcended nature. Even this cursory reflection brings home to us the scale of temporal flow when we consider human beings and nature as their environment. In the past people thought little of themselves within nature, but somewhere along the way they very gradually boosted their position in nature's scheme of things. Now none would deny that human beings dominate nature and are its ruler. The concepts of the deification of human beings and the death of god emerge at this point. So we must acknowledge and give full consideration to the significance of the fact that the portrayal of gods in human form occurred quite some time after the dawn of history.

The first time that human supremacy came to the fore in the West would have been in ancient Greece. The most superior creature in nature should be used to represent the supernatural, and in myths and Greek epic poems the gods are portrayed in human form. Prior to that the lion or eagle, for example, had been used in sculptures as the most beautiful creatures in nature, but in ancient Greece human beings were used for the first time. Arguably, this was the first occasion on which humans became aware of themselves as the ruler of nature. In Japanese and Chinese myths that embody ancient memories, the transcendent beings that correspond to gods are all portrayed in animal form, whereas in relatively recent stories supernatural beings are portrayed in human form. The discussion so far constitutes the first stage of my argument.

NATURE AND THE TECHNOLOGY-MEDIATED ENVIRONMENT

As noted above, people initially used animals to represent gods, but then gradually came to represent them in human form. This was because their intellectual faculties enabled human beings to attain gradual dominance in nature. The human world has a history, and human beings' position in nature has shifted over these long years. People have also changed their own form within nature.

Just looking at a single ancient urn is highly instructive. Take, for instance, urns unearthed in Egypt, or the papyrus paintings found in the Pyramids. Some show people tilling their fields. Most of these people are naked and barefoot, and they hold a whip and are using cows and horses. Since the dawn of recorded history people have had no fear in putting animals to work for them. This is obviously quite a different attitude from that of primitive people, who before the beginning of recorded history drew incantatory paintings deep within caves so as not to be overpowered by animals, and who deliberately performed ceremonies before fearfully setting off on a hunt. Yet surely the naked men using cows to till their fields seem to us to belong to very remote times.

Today we use machinery to plough the fields. Even if we use horses and cattle, we are no longer barefoot. Although human beings have undergone such changes, horses and cattle remain unchanged since olden times. Cows look just the same as four or five thousand years ago. Formerly offered to the gods, these animals have declined in status and are now looked on as a source of labour. In fact, in cities cows are merely regarded as a source of leather, meat and milk. They have the same status in our lives as plants such as vegetables and as trees that are simply used for their materials. Cows are regarded as mere sources of nutrition and material. No longer are they even a helpmeet for our work.

Except for humans, all other living creatures apparently retain the same form as in the past. It is only humans that have changed—in their clothing, in how they work, in how they have created machines and use them to till the fields. Animals, which have remained unchanged, are used only as a backup when the equipment breaks down or as a substitute when people are so poor that they cannot even afford such equipment. Generally speaking, animals are used only as food. Nature is regarded as an imperfect machine.

This means that creatures other than human beings do not possess a history in the strict sense of the term. Animals have no history, just a generational change. They simply undergo changes in the generations. Since the cows in existence today are the descendants of cows from thousands and tens of thousands of years ago, there have undoubtedly been generational changes. With human beings, not only are there generational changes, but also a history. When we consider the relationship between human beings and nature as their environment, we realize that over the course of history human beings have gradually improved their status in nature. In the process their relationship with nature has undergone a change. In my view this is a clear manifestation of the history of the human race.

This is a crucial issue. Although there might be changes in nature—such as evolution and devolution within a biological framework (for example, large primeval creatures such as lizards have become smaller because of the deterioration in their food sources and the climate) and natural changes in distribution, for instance—the only living creatures with a history that cannot be explained in terms of natural dimensions are human beings.

Of course in primeval times human beings did not occupy the lowest rung in nature, but nor did they have a particularly high position. Somewhere along the way they came to occupy the dominant position in nature and a level similar to the people in Egyptian paintings who used cows, once revered as gods, for farming purposes. People are turning our very environment into something unnatural—i.e., a technological environment premised on geometrical forms. In other words, humans are creating various machines that have structures totally inconceivable in nature and are trying to bring nature under their complete control. Human beings not only occupy the dominant position in nature, but are also overpowering it and interposing machinery between nature and themselves. Through technology we have tried to conquer nature as our environment.

The above is a potted history of the human race, which has taken a revolutionary leap in its position within nature. During that time some animals have become extinct, and those that have survived are merely replicating their ancient ecology. Since antiquity zebras have been unable to defeat lions, and their manner of attack has also remained unchanged since primeval times—i.e., zebras don't make tools, but form groups and kick the lion from behind. Yet once human beings can overpower nature with machines, nature's order is gradually destroyed. For reasons of space, I have focused here on periods that particularly stand out—i.e., from prehistory, the era of ancient cave paintings, and from recorded history, ancient Egypt and Japan's mythological era—and compared them with our contemporary times. This shows that human beings were initially submerged in nature but gradually strengthened themselves and sought a position transcending nature. They were able to achieve this through the cognitive faculties with which human beings have been endowed, but more specifically it was because they interposed machines between themselves and nature. For instance, even for such basic tasks as ploughing the fields, tractors are now used. Just what can we learn from the advent of machines? With this we move on to the third stage of our discussion.

What kind of world do we experience today when we leave the house? To be sure, there is air, and also sunlight, so in that sense we move within nature. But what I walk on when I go to university is not earth, but paved roads. What I travel in is a car and a train made by human beings. From that perspective, we can no longer consider nature as our sole environment, as I have repeatedly pointed out in the preceding chapters. It is true that nature constituted our environment in the past, but today we have an additional environment. This is a series of technological environments, such as asphalt and railroad tracks, traffic signals, and the phone—i.e., the technology-mediated environment. It is important to realize that this technology-mediated environment also constitutes an environment. The technology-mediated environment is a concept I presented to the academic world three decades ago using the French term *conjunction technologique*, and nowadays it is used both in Japan and abroad. What this technology-mediated environment consists of is systems that enable us to make our life more convenient. It is precisely because of the existence of the technology-mediated environment that we can drink cold water even in summer despite a lack of rainfall, and that we can have heating on cold days. We can talk by phone with people far away, which is extremely useful. The natural state of affairs was inadequate for ensuring a decent quality of life, so human beings invented machines. The technology-mediated environment consists of a world in which these machines interact, and together with nature this constitutes our everyday environment. That is why *eco-ethica* becomes necessary.

So we need to be fully cognizant of the fact that 'human beings and their environment' cannot be mentally equated with 'human beings and nature'. At first I had indeed thought that we might be able to discuss this by substituting 'human beings and their environment' for 'human beings and nature', but from this third stage on we are forced to conclude that nature is one part of the human environment today and that the technology-mediated environment is also a part of our environment. Of course, there is no question that nature is part of our environment and that the air, sunlight and the earth are indispensable to us. Nevertheless, a moment's reflection on our day-to-day lives shows that we cannot discuss our environment without taking the technology-mediated environment into account.

Not everyone is interested in housing, but anyone who is looking for a house says it has to have a good environment and thinks about wind direction and the availability of water. If you had lived in the countryside in the olden days you would have given careful thought to the environment—whether there was a river nearby, whether the house was on an elevation, whether it faced south, whether there was a grove of trees nearby, and whether other villages were within walking distance. Our environment was solely a question of nature.

But what about today? No matter how fantastic the view might be from your elevated site, if you hear that a major company has bought the land in front of you, you are bound to wonder whether it will put up a tall building and spoil the view. You also have to check out the availability of city gas and train transportation, whether there is any smoke pollution in the area, and so on.

So even when considering our housing environment in very basic terms, we need to take into account not only nature but also the technology-mediated environment. Public facilities such as schools and hospitals are all part of the technology-mediated environment, so it is obvious just how important this is in our overall environment. Even if a building has the drawback of facing north, as long as various equipment is provided—e.g., a powerful air conditioner, air-purifying equipment, and double-glazed windows to block out noise—this might be better than a south-facing house that lacks such facilities. When deciding on a house we also consider questions such as whether there is car parking space and an expressway nearby. All this shows just how important is the technology-mediated environment, along with the natural environment, in our everyday lives. So when we talk of 'human beings and nature', we cannot simply think of 'human beings and their environment' in clear-cut terms, but must think along the lines of 'human beings and a particular aspect of their environment'. And we must acknowledge that the technology-mediated environment has become a crucial element in our lives. We also need to reconsider the true essence of human beings.

Up until now human beings and nature had been thought to stand in opposition to each other. We must now ask for the first time whether human beings belong to the technology-mediated environment or to nature. We are forced to the conclusion that no matter how much human beings might use codes, and even if they merely exist and move within a planned system, they are not machines in the technology-mediated environment. In view of their essence, human beings belong to nature.

We are indisputably part of nature. So at this stage of the discussion we have verified the following facts, although perhaps they were evident from the outset: (1) our environment consists not only of nature, but also the technology-mediated environment, and if we were to ask which of these two environments human beings belong to—i.e., nature or the technology-mediated environment—then (2) we are part of nature. So this means that even though human beings are part of nature and are creatures living in nature—i.e., we are merely nature—at some time or other we transformed ourselves into an entity distinct from nature and superior to other elements of nature, by creating objects that are distinct from ourselves. Although this is an obvious point, the technology-mediated environment was originally nothing more than a weapon as a tool for human beings. Objects used as tools were combined and at some stage took on a greater role, becoming elevated in status to an environment for human beings. Is it ethical to assimilate to this environment?

By rights, we should explore a whole range of issues related to the technology-mediated environment, but one aspect in particular needs clarification—i.e., the attribute of the technology-mediated environment that distinguishes it from the natural environment. In other words, where does the essence of the technology-mediated environment reside? Of course, this environment has many different aspects, but the simplest image would be the mountain-climbing and cable car analogy mentioned earlier. Alpinism still exists today, but mountain-climbing involves a flesh-and-blood—i.e., natural—person slogging up a steep mountain out there in nature. Climbing a three- or four-thousand metre mountain on foot requires setting aside several days, but with a cable car you can get to the summit in ten or fifteen minutes. It is true that cable cars offer wonderful advantages. For example, if an elderly person who is ill wants, before dying, to go up a mountain they climbed long ago in their youth, they can be taken up by cable car, which is indeed a great boon. Thanks to the cable car, even children with polio who had never imagined climbing a mountain can enjoy the view from up in the mountains. So we must acknowledge that the technology-mediated environment has indeed brought great benefits. It has the ethical potential to serve the weak.

At times we might want to take a break from our busy lives and breathe in the clean mountain air and relax up there for a few days. If on the first half day we reach the bottom of the cable car run and ascend from there, a morning departure will get us to a hotel on top of the mountain by evening. We can spend two or three days there before heading back home. If we climbed the mountain under our own steam, there is no way we could recharge our batteries in that brief time. So cable cars can be regarded as a wonderful aid indeed. Yet we need to consider the essence of the workings of the technology-mediated environment, as symbolized by the cable car.

I would suggest, as discussed in the previous chapter, that this essence consists of a completely new form of abstraction. What do I mean by this? Abstraction refers to the act of extracting something. For instance, when dozens of people are present in a room, there will be a range of ages amongst them. Let us set aside these age-based differences—i.e., abstract age from our considerations, so that age is not taken into account. Instead we focus solely, for instance, on those people in the group who are (or are not) wearing glasses. If we focus on the fact of wearing glasses, only those with glasses are included. The act of setting a particular goal and focusing on (abstracting) just certain aspects and discarding (eliminating) all other aspects is known as abstraction. So abstraction and elimination are carried out simultaneously.

In the past logical abstraction was the only form of abstraction, but the technology-mediated environment has led to the appearance of technological abstraction. In other words, what technology does is minimize the processes and shorten the passage of time as much as possible and, if feasible, eliminate this passage altogether and abstract just the outcome. One example of such abstraction is the industrialization of food, as in canned and frozen food products, for instance. The process of individuals preparing food is eliminated, and only the end product of meals is abstracted. The convenience of this derives from the large-scale socialization of individuals' lifestyles. Even those non-work-related parts of life where individuals' tastes come freely to the fore are given a monetary twist and become a commercial operation. This could be interpreted as economic efficiency leading to the spread of corporatization across the entire spectrum of human behaviour, and as the beginning of technology-enabled corporate infiltration into individuals' behaviour. Already this presents an occasion for questioning corporate ethics, but let us move on, since our focus here is on the theme of nature. In short, even the temporal latitude or leisure that individuals gain from this situation—i.e., even their completely free time—becomes a corporate target.

This is a major problem that has an impact on nature. Since there are indeed limits to what individuals can do, when travelling, for instance, group tours are more efficient. Travel in ancient China used to be a major collective undertaking requiring the building of bridges and roads, and in both the East and the West pilgrimages such as thanks-giving pilgrimages were often done in groups. Today, when sightseeing has been corporatized, large planes and buses have reshaped and destroyed nature to the point that the very landscape has been transformed, and hotels and holiday home companies monopolize the views. Rather than legal regulations, what is needed is a revolution in awareness through *eco-ethica*. These problems too are caused in the first place by a new form of abstraction that compresses the passage of time without awaiting *Zeitigung* (the unfolding of time).

Shrinking the passage of time involves two aspects: (1) labour-saving—i.e., eliminating effort on the part of humans, and (2) time-saving. As a result of these two aspects the outcome is abstracted—a phenomenon I refer to as technological abstraction. I am not saying this is good or bad. In fact, it has both positive and negative aspects. Let's look at the negative side. To take the mountain-climbing example, strength or weakness of body is no longer an issue. As long as people have money for the cable car fee, anyone can go up to the summit. So the cable car means that the virtues of effort, endurance and teamwork fostered through alpinism are not cultivated in the course of ascending the mountain. All that remains is the outcome—i.e., the view from the top. The resulting elimination of human effort and the reduction in the time needed are major characteristics of the technology-mediated environment. Although this admittedly has very convenient and positive aspects, it is essential to be aware also of the negative aspects above.

Just what constitutes the essence of human beings? We must conclude that the essence of human existence lies in awareness, because we are not held to account for matters of which we were unaware. If in our everyday lives we get drunk and abuse our boss, as long as we humbly apologize, saying we are very sorry because we had too much to drink the night before, we will sometimes be forgiven because we were not ourselves. Our words will be regarded as having been spoken while we were heavily intoxicated and unaware of what we were saying, and we are forgiven because people are not held liable for their unconscious behaviour. So, as conscious beings, we forgive ourselves and others.

Although our bodies are extremely important to us, this illustrates just how vital is our awareness, which is what makes us truly human. If someone were unfortunate enough to lose his right arm in an accident or had to have an operation on one lung, so that his physical appearance and form underwent a complete transformation, we might say that he looks different, but we would not say that he has changed. Yet if someone turns into a completely serious person one day, they are described as having changed, no matter how outwardly unchanged they might appear. From this we must conclude that it is awareness that constitutes the essential element of human existence. This awareness that is the human essence is formed and developed over time. In other words, awareness is a temporal entity, just as philosophical tradition has argued. The major question then becomes whether the compression of time through technology leads to a compression of awareness, which is the essence of human beings, who are a temporal existence.

LEARNING FROM NATURE

Admittedly, as acknowledged earlier, the technology-mediated environment is bringing us numerous benefits, but in many tasks it also compresses time as much as possible and promotes labour-saving. Although this 'saving of labour' is convenient in eliminating physical effort, it tends to deprive us of the effort and perseverance involved in striving to do our utmost. This suggests that the technology-mediated environment as an environment for human beings is a place where labour-saving occurs, the time needed to complete tasks is compressed, and virtues such as perseverance are lost. To put it another way, it is a realm where elements that are the proper province of awareness are erased as much as possible. There is a dehumanization through detemporalization.

So what kind of entity is nature? Just now I said that the technology-mediated environment is something that minimizes time as much as possible and saves labour, but what about nature? Well, nature is imbued with a waiting stance. Nature requires waiting. The technology-mediated environment attempts to produce results as quickly as possible, and in contemporary society this is feasible to some degree. In nature, however, nightingales do not sing in that sweet voice until the arrival of spring. They wait for spring, burst forth in song, and breed. Once the eggs are laid, they have to be incubated for several days or they won't hatch. The chicks don't become parents until a year has passed. Natural processes can probably be expedited somewhat in the technology-mediated environment. So today we can eat cucumbers in any season, and we can enjoy strawberries all year round. If we build hothouses and create an eternal spring or eternal summer, it is possible to eat seasonal fruit and vegetables at any time of the year at all. Even so, strawberries require a certain time for the seeds to turn into seedlings and to grow and produce fruit. Even in the technology-mediated environment, therefore, nature desperately protects such temporality.

Earlier I stated that human beings are in essence a part of nature. And compared with other creatures in nature we are an entity that has a need to stress the temporality of awareness. Stressing temporality means emulating nature's waiting stance. This fosters the patience to await the unfolding of time, as well as an awareness of waiting.

Like it or not, today we could be regarded as creatures rushing about in the technology-mediated environment—as beings in motion. This environment facilitates our work, so we obtain the fruits of this as an inevitable outcome of the assembly line. Still dissatisfied with this, however, we want to produce more things more quickly, and in no time the technology-mediated environment that originally evolved so as to give us more free time has turned into a high-speed society. Here I am not referring only to the speed of cars or planes. Our everyday lives are moving at a dizzying pace. In the technology-mediated environment that consists of this high-speed society we have come to regard waiting as a necessary evil. Yet surely we should be able to wait for artificial organs to be developed?

When matters reach this point, we need to stop and remember that we are part of nature and nature is something that awaits maturation, that waits for the time to be ripe. We must realize that nature is not just material for us to exploit or matter for us to conquer, but that it is also our teacher. This realization leads to an attitude of learning from nature. No doubt people spoke of these things in the old days, but it is time for us to consider the true meaning of learning from nature. By no means does it simply provide us with resources or our environment. We must recapture the attitude of learning humbly from nature and regarding it as our teacher. And, in my view, this is what will in fact happen. So let us move on to the fourth idea.

Earlier I said we cannot equate 'human beings and their environment' with 'human beings and nature'. Nature is just one part of our environment. Yet when we compared it with the technology-mediated environment that constitutes another part of our environment, we were forced to conclude that human beings belong to nature. We must not forget that we ourselves are creatures of nature. In terms of the attitude that we, as an element of nature, have adopted toward other elements of nature, in the past we simply regarded nature as mere resources, as something to be conquered. Yet we need to look on other elements of nature as teaching us how to live. In some respects nature must take on the role of our teacher. So although of course the goals of preserving and protecting nature aim at satisfying aesthetic demands and looking after the health of urban-dwellers, these goals must also include reviving in our lives that which we have forgotten—i.e., the meaning of making our inner selves truly calm and the meaning of waiting. In this way the idea of protecting nature also has ethical grounds.

Let's pause to consider the meaning of endurance. Here I am not referring to the feudal concept of endurance. We should remember that one aspect of nature is its role as a teacher that reminds us of the meaning of waiting and enduring. *Eco-ethica* is an ethics that learns from nature.

Just as we give gifts to our elderly teachers and help them out in their day-to-day activities, surely we should also think about looking after nature, which in some respects has been our teacher from of old but which is today being cast aside. Nowadays there is much talk of protecting nature, but it is driven solely by such worldly reasons as the fact that pollution is a major problem and nature's beauty is being despoiled and the landscape degraded, or the fact that our health will suffer or disasters will occur if nature is destroyed. Although these are all important issues and I am not gainsaying them, they alone are not sufficient. In other words, to truly make the most of that aspect of ourselves whereby we become part of nature and are creatures of nature, what is vital is the ethical attitude of learning from nature and valuing our teacher in this. I would particularly like to stress the importance of such an attitude when considering the topic of human beings and nature. Science too represents the outcome of learning from how nature has manifested itself.

Numerous issues surface when the question of human beings and nature is reexamined from such a perspective. Nowadays many people believe that human beings reign supreme in nature, and they accept this as an incontrovertible reality. Yet if human reproduction is considered, we notice something truly odd. Human beings are without doubt one of the most outstanding creatures in nature and undeniably the creature that forms the most powerful groups, but it should be noted that our most biologically advanced attribute is sex. In human beings, sex is a double-edged sword—it is an energy that animates life while simultaneously harboring the potential for sin if this inner need is mishandled.

No matter how much culture or technology might advance, a single human being alone is utterly incapable of even giving birth to the next generation. Amazingly, in some lower species a single creature can produce the next generation by itself. In other words, some animals are hermaphrodites, and even a single flower is capable of producing the next generation because it has stamens and a pistil. But when we think of human beings as a part of nature—i.e., human beings who are not machines (machines can't give birth to offspring) and who are part of nature and are capable of giving birth—and of sex as their reproductive force, we realize that individuals have an absolute need for a partner in order for sex to fulfill its function and have meaning. So when we talk of people as relational beings, it would be more appropriate to describe them as dependent in the sense of needing or awaiting an other. Human beings truly are an other-waiting (inter-reliant) creature. Because we are interdependent, sex too can become either a life force or sin.

The individual is indeed a being of dignity with great value, but as far as nature is concerned, even reproduction—i.e., producing the next generation—is something that individuals are totally incapable of achieving alone. Human beings are an other-waiting (interdependent) creature that must await another sex. This applies not only to having children. Joint efforts by men and women are necessary for various kinds of creation. Human beings are sexual beings that must perforce rely on other individuals. It is precisely for the sake of psychological creation that sex relies on the opposite sex.

To put it another way, no matter how many convenient devices we acquire in our technology-mediated environment and how much stronger than the group we might feel, human beings are truly no more than creatures that rely on others—i.e., inter-reliant beings. So even with just the single phenomenon of human reproduction, the essence of nature, which consists of waiting, can indeed be found in human beings. This is why *eco-ethica* insists on the dialogic inter-reliance of human beings.

No matter how much one might pride oneself as a human being, the human self is helpless on its own. Human beings undoubtedly occupy a dominant position in nature in that form, but we need to become aware of our ephemeral, helpless existence. In *eco-ethica*, individualism lies in the virtue of valuing others as much as oneself.

So again we must look at matters from a broad perspective. We need to think long and hard not just about the question of sex as reproduction and pleasure, but also about what kind of being are individuals undertaking tasks. No doubt Aristotle's words will spring to mind as defining our true nature: "Man is a polis-like animal." 'Polis' refers to the Greek city-state and is generally translated as 'the state' or 'society', which leads me to render 'polis-like' as 'state-like' or 'society-like' or 'political' and Aristotle's statement as 'Man is a social animal' or 'Man is a political animal'. Yet originally this meant an animal that must form groups to survive. So although human beings are individuals, when undertaking a task we cannot be isolated like a scorpion. Human beings live as pack animals—i.e., as beings that depend on others, as inter-reliant beings, we form political organizations.

Since humans are inter-reliant beings in this way, we need to help each other in order to survive. For instance, in the world of politics we hear of democracy, the politics of the *demos* (the people). In line with this principle, people who cannot make it alone form a group, then as many as possible give voice to their opinions on the group's common interests and common demands, and the direction of politics is determined accordingly.

But if we fail to observe nature carefully, we might confuse this democracy with democratism. I believe that democracy is a mistake. Without elaboration, this will seem an outrageous statement, but nowhere does the word *democracy* contain the meaning of *democratism*. *Democracy* refers to *democratic politics*, and this is indeed necessary for human beings as an inter-reliant existence, as stated earlier. But *democratism* is different from *democracy*. *Democratism* is the idea of deciding everything by the majority.

A look at the world of nature shows that groups of animals in the wild always exhibit leadership. There are animals that are expert lookouts, for instance, and they take turns in standing guard, and even if a large group gets unruly, they hold firm. And when the group is on the move, there is a leader, as well as mid-ranking animals that are in charge of the rear guard. This hierarchy excludes democratism and does not entail deciding everything in line with the demands of the majority. In disputes, the leader imposes its own judgment. Does this mean the leader is a despot? Animals in nature are on the whole extremely harmonious, and their way of life involves taking the group's demands on board according to the hierarchy. With some species there is a convention whereby the leader loses its position in a fight once its powers of command have waned. This is the case with monkeys, and the same goes for lions and fur seals. There are other species where a leader that has lost its strength leaves the group and goes off to die.

In nature, therefore, there is a clear distinction between democracy and democratism. In the case of human beings, democracy means that in the political arena each person has equal rights and an equal position and states what he or she wants. And the majority will prevail. This is restricted, however, to the political arena.

To give a farfetched example, with democratism someone might say "My cancer is just not getting any better, so the doctor must be in the wrong. Let's decide by national referendum what kind of treatment would be best." Nobody would listen if that happened. The same goes for the arts. Only connoisseurs are appointed arbiters of the arts. If non-connoisseurs say they like a picture, they will be told that they don't understand art and this is just their personal taste. The pronouncements of connoisseurs are underpinned by aesthetic theory. So democratism is something that should not by rights exist, yet somewhere along the way people got the idea that everyone is equal in ability, because in the technology-mediated environment everyone has the potential to produce a similar outcome, no matter how weak they might be. Equality of character and inequality in ability are fundamental propositions in *eco-ethica*.

For instance, if one were to run from Tokyo to Hakone as if in a marathon, the strong would win, but in a technological society people don't do this. They take a train, and no matter how fast you might run in the carriage it makes no difference. You can sit down for the ride, so it's all the same whether you have a bad leg or are a marathon athlete. We tend toward democratism in all domains, because we think that differences in ability are invisible. Yet these differences are obvious in our work, and if we fail to value such differences human beings will be reduced to cogs in a machine. Inter-reliant human beings, however, all have different abilities.

We must humbly take another look at nature and learn how much we need to cooperate in nature, as well as just how necessary competition is. Competition inevitably produces winners and losers. Yet winning and losing merely indicate differences in ability and luck. In terms of moral character, everyone is the same. To promote democracy (democratic politics) in the true sense, therefore, we must abolish democratism. Becoming accustomed to this in the technology-mediated environment means we risk losing sight of it. We need to rethink what the ethics of learning from nature entails in this respect. In order to defend democracy, *eco-ethica* rejects democratism.

So far we have examined the theme of human beings and nature in terms of an opposition between nature and human beings, or as a single unit, but in closing we should recall that human beings have an inherent aspect that ultimately transcends nature. Though part of nature, we also have an intrinsically supranatural aspect. I believe this is a question of the human intellect, or perhaps we could call it spirituality. Born as flesh and blood, human beings truly possess something natural, and movement is also natural. Yet by no means do we consist solely of nature. Remember that creatures that consisted solely of nature did not possess a history. Human beings have created history precisely because we have an awareness that continually strives to transcend our natural self. Although we might have made many mistakes in history, human greatness lies in the fact that we have created history and continue to do so even today.

Elsewhere in nature there are just generational changes, with no aspiration to rise above nature, so no history. Human beings, on the other hand, seek to surpass nature, always striving to transcend their given environment. Transcending one's environment entails feeling a sense of lack. A lack is an absence—i.e., nothingness. Being human involves discovering phenomenological nothingness as a lack and striving to reach existential fulfilment in that respect. Even if we approach existential fulfilment, we again discover a lack there and try to overcome this. This transcendental orientation is the source of ethics.

In other words, human beings are endlessly seeking existential fulfilment. This means we have the attribute of moving toward existence itself—i.e., toward an existence without nothingness. Existence itself, complete fulfilment—such an absolute does not exist in this world. If I might preempt my conclusion, we are a *god-like being*. Human beings have the attribute of seeking a philosophical existence that is inferior to God. Our very existence is ultimately supranatural. Human beings are a creature of nature that reaches out toward a supranatural entity. We must not forget that human beings are both a part of nature and inclined toward the supranatural.

It is only when we ponder on such matters—i.e., only when we look at things from a supranatural perspective—that issues such as human sin or goodness can be considered in the true sense. It would be safe to say that there is no sin in ordinary nature. Even if evil exists in the animal world, there is no sin. In this way are woven the fundamental issues of *eco-ethica*.

In my opinion, the fact that human sin can be thought of in this way is related to how we are a part of nature while also being linked to the supranatural. In other words, by comparing ourselves with the perfect Absolute, we come to a realization of our internal sin as our own emptiness and ugliness. In order to live as a human being, then, there have been two approaches to transcending nature as our environment—i.e., the technological and metaphysical approaches. Today, when the technology-mediated environment has become a part of our environment, we need a strong awareness that the arts and *eco-ethica* exist in order for us to transcend this technology-mediated environment.

Invitees to the International Symposium on Eco-ethica

R. Klibansky, P. Ricœur, M. Dufrenne, J. Parain-Vial, J. Margolis, E. zum Brunn, and B. Koh are longstanding honored members, and they have participated in the Symposium from time to time. P. McCormick, M. Olivetti, P. Kemp, R. Bernasconi, and N. Hashimoto are core members, while J. Simon, F. Jacques, J. Kuçuradi, H. Boeder and J. Mosterin participate as leading philosophers from the West and M. Jung, K. Paik, M. Dy, T. Doan, L. Garcia, and B. Sugiharto attend as leading philosophers from the East. Kōichi Tsujimura, Kunitake Itō, Ryōsuke Inagaki, Isao Toshimitsu, Megumi Sakabe, and Hisamitsu Miyauchi have been frequent Japanese invitees. The first twenty-three symposia were held in Japan, but since 2004 the Symposium has been held in Copenhagen every year. This has been successful thanks to the great efforts on the part of the chair, Professor P. Kemp. This initiative has led to the involvement of Scandinavian scholars—D. Rasmussen, J. Rendorff, and B. Uggla—and young scholars from Central Europe—P. Chardel and B. Rebber.

Due to space limitations, I have listed only those scholars who have been invited on three or more occasions. The Symposium is always limited to a maximum of twenty participants. It is a very intense gathering where participants devote themselves to discussion from early morning until the middle of the night over a period of six days. After each Symposium a proceedings totaling around 200 pages is published.

Index

abortion, 6, 69
absence, ix, 5, 92
abstraction, ix, 65–67, 84–85; new form of, ix, 65, 84, 85; technological, 65–67, 85
acts performed at the behest of machines, 8
aesthetics, 9, 67
AIDS, 22
Altamira, 77
Analects, 39
animals, 1, 60, 61, 70, 77, 81, 89; gods represented as, 78, 79, 80; humans as, 11, 90; representations of, 77–78, 80; of the same species, 60, 61; skilled, 26–29
aretology, vii, viii, 34
Aristotle, 11, 41, 62, 63, 64, 90; cardinal virtues of, 4, 33; *Nicomachean Ethics* of, 41, 50, 62–63; premises of, 13, 64, 66. See also *eutrapelia*; syllogism of action
art galleries, 16
art works, 16, 77
arti ethica, viii
artificial organs, ix, 69, 87
artificial physical structure, 12
austerity, 66
awareness, vii, 4, 7, 9, 14, 15, 18, 36, 42, 49, 54, 92; as the essence of human existence, 67, 86; ethical, viii, 9, 15; revolution in, 37, 85; as a temporal entity, 86, 87. See also consciousness

babies, pros and cons of choosing the sex of, 22
barometer of iniquity, 30
beasts, 78, 79
beggars, 41
behavioral controls, 16
behavioral guidelines, 21
behavioral norms, vii, 15,
behavioral responses, semiotic 11
behaviour, 18, 23, 28, 42, 55, 56, 61; human, 12, 23, 85; regulated by machines, 7, 8; and responsibility, 43, 86; sphere of, 25–26, 52. See also society, behaviour in
benevolence, 25, 33
Berlinger, Rudolph, ix, 10
betrayal, 9, 27, 55
Bible, 19, 63
bioethics, viii, 1, 22
birth-control measures, 6
Boeder, H., 93
boorishness, 50, 54
bourgeoisie, 35
brain death, ix, 69

Buddha, 25
buffoonery, 50
burial mound figures, 34
bushidō, 28, 44

cable cars, 66, 84, 85
capital, large, 64
cars, 16, 18, 51, 58, 87
categorical imperatives of religion, 5
cave paintings, 77, 78, 81
Centre International pour Étude Comparée de Philosophie et d'Esthètique, xii, 2, 17
Christ, 25, 41, 43
Christian ethics, 33, 41
Christianity, 4, 6, 7, 22, 33, 36, 42
Chuang-Tzu, 57
citizens, 8, 31, 36, 41, 45
collective responsibility, 64
committees, 14, 23, 53, 64, 65
communal raising of children, 35
communications, 26, 51, 58
compassion, 25
compression of time, 86
computers, 26, 68
concepts, 7, 11, 43, 44, 49, 79
Confucian ethics, 6, 7, 25, 28, 33, 39, 40
Confucianism, 6, 7, 33
Confucius, 25, 39, 40
connoisseurs, 91
consciousness, 7, 25, 44, 49, 66; revolution in, 56, 57, 72. *See also* awareness; moral consciousness
convenience, 5, 8, 16, 40, 85
corporate ethics, 72, 85
cosmopolitanism, 46–49
courage, 4, 28, 33, 37–38, 52, 66
covenant bond, 36
cultural assets, 17, 29, 40
culture, vii, viii, 3, 7, 8, 9, 31, 37, 44, 53, 89; and technology, 15, 26, 28, 89; as a pastime, 7–8; as self-development, 7–8
cybernetics, 19

Da Vinci, Leonardo, 29

decency, human, 29
decision-making, 13, 14, 60, 64, 65
democracy, 90–91
democratism, 90–91
Descartes, 42
dialogic inter-reliance, 89
differences in ability, 91
dignity, human, 20, 51, 68, 69, 89
discipline, 9, 39
discrimination, 3, 35, 36
divine salvation, 36
Dufrenne, Mikel, 93
dying for one's country, 20, 33
dynamis (potentiality), 12

eco, 1–2
eco-ethica, v, vi, vi, xii, 1, 3, 10, 14, 23, 30, 31, 33, 55, 69, 71, 72, 82, 85, 89, 91; aims of, vi, 10, 11, 29, 49, 92; constructing, ix, 49; essence of, viii, 1–3, 88; in our day-to-day lives, 29–31; new discipline of, v–vi; origins of the term, 1–2, 7; scope of, 16, 28, 76; symposia on, v, ix, xi, xii, 2; topics in, viii, 5, 16, 23, 55, 91
ecological changes, 7, 17
ecology, 1, 21, 81
economic efficiency, 85
education: communal, 35; moral, 9, 51, 54. *See also* ethics, teaching of
effectiveness, 12, 21, 24, 51, 56, 61, 64, 66; technological, 16, 25
efficiency, 8, 85
effort, viii, 6, 16, 26, 28, 35, 38, 45, 54, 89; elimination of human, 85, 86
egoism, vi, 21, 35, 69
Egypt, 80, 81
Egyptian sculptures, 78
electricity, vi, 17, 21, 58, 63, 70, 73
elevators, 65
elite, 7, 45
Emperor Jimmu, 77
Emperor Meiji, 34
endurance, 85, 88
energeia (actuality), 12

Index

energy, 13, 20, 70, 73, 89. *See also* nuclear power
engineering technology, 21
environment, vi, vii, 5, 6, 14, 15, 17, 18, 29, 37, 57, 62, 68; and human relations, 11, 40. *See also* natural environment; technology-mediated environment
environmental ethics, viii, 1, 14
equality, 3, 6, 7, 36, 49, 66, 91
erasure of moral character, 58, 59
essence of human existence, 42, 67, 83, 86, 87
ethica, 7. *See also* eco-ethica; ethics; *ethica ad faciem*; *ethica ad hominem*; *ethica ad rem*; *ethica facie ad faciem*; *meta-ethica*; *techno-ethica*
ethical responsibility, vii, 16
ethical systems, viii, 1, 23, 33, 34
ethics, 2, 3, 7, 8, 10, 13, 15, 16, 18, 21, 23, 28, 29, 30, 31, 42, 43, 45, 48, 61, 62, 70, 71; changes in, 36, 37; core of, 5, 10, 43, 92; as a discipline, v, ix, 2, 9, 11, 15, 23, 38, 71; formulation of, 7, 35; as human engineering, 62, 68; individual, 65; issues in, 4, 22; and nature, 88, 91; new, v, vi, vii, xi, 1, 5, 10, 13, 22, 29, 31, 33, 34, 49, 63, 73; progress in, 26, 37, 38; and religion, 25, 36; restoration of, 5, 15, 31, 46, 67; scholars of, ix, 2–3, 9, 29, 44, 71, 93; scope of, vii, 12, 15, 22; sexual, 6; spatial, 50; system of, 33, 49; teaching of, 9, 21, 28, 71; temporal, 50, 51; traditional, viii, 11, 12, 13, 14, 25, 33, 50. *See also* aretology; bioethics; Christian ethics; Confucian ethics; corporate ethics; environmental ethics; *ethica*; ethics toward things; face-to-face ethics; group ethics; interpersonal ethics; medical ethics; philosophical ethics; work ethics
ethics toward things (*ethica ad rem*), vii, viii, 15, 16

eutrapelia (mental diversion), 46, 50
evil, ix, 30, 69, 87, 92
existential fulfillment, 92
existentialism, 42
extramarital sex, 22

face-to-face ethics (*ethica ad faciem*), 25
face-to-face ethics (*ethica facie ad faciem*), 12
faith, 4, 5, 33, 35, 38
faithfulness, 39
family, 2, 6, 34, 35, 36, 51, 54
fascism, 18
fax, 26, 58
fealty, 38, 39
fidelity, 33
freedom of thought, 20
Freud, Sigmund, 35
friendship, 66
functional sociological relations, 11

Gabriel, Leo, 2
generational change, 80, 81, 92
genetic (DNA) manipulation, 22, 51
genitals, 22, 70
Giedion, Siegfried, 78
global warming, 16
god, 19, 29, 35, 36, 41, 70, 80, 81, 92; becoming one with, 63, 64; Christian, 5, 36; Greek, 70, 77, 79; Japanese, 70, 77, 79; representations of, 78–80
godfathers, 48, 49
golden kite, 77
good, 9, 38, 67, 68, 92
Greek mythology, 70, 79
greetings, 60, 61
group ethics, vi, 14, 65
group tours, 85
Griebendorf, 9

Häckel, Ernst, 1
Hare, Richard Mervyn, 9
Heinemann, F. H., 42
Hellenism, 48

history, 4, 15, 22, 40, 78; of animals, 80, 92; of art, 9; of creating virtues, 34–45; dawn of, 6, 76, 79, 80; of ethical thought, 9, 10, 34; of the human race, 26, 37, 57, 80, 81, 92; Japanese, 44; prehistory, 77, 78, 81; recorded, 4, 76, 80, 81
Homer, 8, 41
homosexuals, 22
hope, 4, 5, 33, 64
human essence, 42, 67, 83, 86, 87
human habitat, changes in, 11, 13, 14, 17–18, 21, 67, 76, 80
humans (*anthropos*), 11
humans-as-machines concept, 19
humility, vii, 40–42
humour, 50
Husserl, Edmund, 11

iki, 44
illegitimate children, 34, 35
Inagaki, Ryōsuke, 93
individualism, 89
inequality in ability, 91
inevitable indirectness, technological, 12
intellect, 27, 91
intellectuals, 5, 7, 45
intercourse, 6, 22, 77
internal erasure, 58, 59
internationalism, 48
interpersonal ethics (*ethica ad hominem*), vii, 15, 28
inter-reliance, 89
Intersubjectivität, 11
Intersubjectivité, 11
ipseity, 49
Israel, people of, 36
Izanagi, 70, 77
Izanami, 70, 77

Jacques, Francis, 93
Japanese mythology, 70, 77
Jung, Myong-hwan, xii
Judaism, 22

junshi, 34
justice, 4, 33, 35, 36
Kagutsuchi, 70
Kanagawa incident, 45
Kant, Immanuel, 43, 49, 68
Katō, Shinrō, 50
Kemp, Peter, 49, 93
kibbutzes, 35
kindness toward foreigners, 45
Klibansky, Raymond, 2, 93
knowledge, 45, 51, 70, 71
Koh, Byong-Ik, 93
Kojiki (Records of Ancient Matters), 8, 44, 77
kosmopolites (citizen of the world), 48
Kritik der Praktischen Vernunft, 43

labour-saving, 8, 19, 59, 66, 85, 86
language, viii, 11, 27, 37, 48–49, 53, 59, 61
Lascaux, 77
Law for the Protection of Cultural Properties, 29
leadership, 90
liberation, 3, 22, 35, 50, 61
libraries, 55–56
life, 5, 19, 21, 23, 38, 59, 61, 67, 69, 76, 82, 85, 90; actual, 35, 56; circumstances, 13, 15; making easier, 48, 49; everyday, 17, 18, 52; forms, 10, 11, 12, 16, 40, 75; force, 69, 89; harming, ix, 23, 73; human, v, viii, ix, 3; meaning of, 20, 21, 69; moral, 29, 42; risking, 19, 20; sacrificing of, 19, 20, 21, 37; sciences, 22, 51, 69; value of, 19, 20, 21; way of, 43, 70, 90
lifestyle, 20, 50, 85
living well (*to eũ zên*), 18–20, 21, 68
logic, viii, ix, 6, 9, 10, 13, 18, 20, 51, 53, 57, 62, 68, 73, 85
logical structure, 13, 62, 64, 65
logical structure of action, 62–64, 66
love, 4, 5, 6, 19, 22, 25, 33, 34, 36, 51, 58, 59; of strangers (see *philoxenia*). See also neighbourly love
loyalty, 33, 38–40, 44, 65

Index

McCormick, Peter, ix, 51, 93
machines, 6, 8, 50, 57, 58, 59, 60, 62, 68, 80, 81, 83; creation of, 80, 81, 82; human beings as, 18, 19, 59, 60, 61, 89, 91; labour-saving, 8, 19; and nature, 80, 81, 82; operation of, 21, 27, 46, 59, 62; regulating people's behaviour, 7, 8, 50; and time, 8–9, 46
McKeon, Richard, 43, 44
management, 12, 71, 72
manliness, 37, 38
Manyōshū, 8
Marcel, Gabriel, 11
Margolis, Joseph, 93
Marx, Karl, 35
means, vi, 8, 13, 19, 51, 63, 64, 65, 66, 68, 73; choice of, 13, 63, 64, 66
mechanistic worldview, 18
medical ethics, 1, 22, 68
medicine, viii, ix, 19, 22, 68, 69, 73
megalopsychia, 41
Meno, 33
meta-ethica, 9
metaphysica, 2, 10
metaphysics, 2, 22
metatechnica, 2, 10
Michelangelo, 29
militarism, 18
military groups, 33
Mill, John Stuart, 44
moderation, 4, 5, 33
monastery, 63
moral character, 36, 49, 59, 91
moral concepts, 44
moral consciousness, 23, 53–62, 72; Japanese, 23, 53–57. See also technology-mediated environment, and changes in moral consciousness
moral principles, 28, 30
moral propositions, 9, 10
moral responsibility, 65
moral theology, 22
moral views, 6
morality: future, 67; historical, 68; public, 16, 55; in terms of the universe, 67, 68
morals, 8, 9, 18, 25, 26, 27, 28, 29, 30, 34, 36, 37, 38, 39, 40, 41, 46, 52, 53, 54, 57, 61; creation of, viii, 30, 40; Japanese, 53, 54, 55, 56, 57; realm of, 40, 46; traffic, 18
moratorium, vi
mottainasa (frugality), 44
museums, 16, 28, 55
mythos of fire, 70, 72, 73

nationalism, vii
natural environment, 2, 11, 15, 17, 25, 75, 76, 79–84, 88, 92
nature, vii, 18, 49, 52, 60, 73, 75–77, 79–92; coexistence with, 15, 76, 77; destruction of, 16, 40, 67, 73, 85, 88; gods of, 70; learning from, 86–92; morality in relation to, 16, 28; protection of, 16, 88; dominance of, vii, 76, 79, 80. *See also* machines, and nature; natural environment; *physis*; technology-mediated environment, and nature
Nature and Man, 75
Nazism, 18
neighbours: distance from, vii, 12, 23–24, 26, 30; rethinking the concept of, 12–14, 24, 51; visibility of, vii, 12
neighbourly love, 5, 24–25, 45, 51
New Testament, 36, 41
Nicomachean Ethics, 41, 50, 62, 63
Nicomachus, 62
Nietzsche, 35, 36
Nihon Shoki, 77
Ningen no gaku toshite no rinrigaku (Ethics as the study of human beings), 15
Nogi, Maresuke, 28, 34
non-physical effectiveness, 12
nosism, vi
nothingness, 92
nuclear power, 12, 67, 70, 71, 72, 73

Odysseus, 41

Old Testament, 5, 36
Olivetti, Marco M., ix, 49, 93
organ transplants, ix, 23, 51, 52, 68, 69
organs, ix, 23, 68, 69, 87
other-waiting creatures, 89

Paik, Ki Soo, 93
papyrus, 80
Parain-Vial, Jean, 2, 93
perception, sphere of, 12, 25, 26
perseverance, 66, 86
personal self-development (*Bildung*), 7
personality, 36
Phidias, 77
philosophers, 22, 23, 25, 36, 44, 69, 72, 93. See also Nietzsche; Plato; Ricœur; Stoic philosophers; Watsuji
philosophical ethics, 20
philosophy, viii, 1, 3, 10, 23, 25, 43, 49, 64, 71, 86, 92; of the city, 2, 10; transformation of, 35, 38. See also Centre International pour Étude Comparée de Philosophie et d'Esthètique; existentialism; *Revue Internationale de Philosophie Moderne*
Philosophy, 64
physica, 2
physical adjustment, 61
physis, 2
Pietà, 29
pilgrimages, thanks-giving, 85
Plato, 19, 33, 34, 35, 36, 51
polis, 33, 90
politeness, 33
Politia (*The Republic*), 34
politica, 10
politics of the *demos* (the people), 90
pollution, 3, 5, 15, 76, 83, 88
Praxiteles, 77
premises, 13, 63, 64 , 66. See also Aristotle, premises of
Princess Ototachibana, 19
production, 4, 8, 12
profits, pursuit of, 12

Prometheus, 70
power, pursuit of, 12
property damage, 29
propositions, 9, 10, 91
punctiliousness (*ponctualité*), 46
punctuality, 46
purpose, 49, 63, 64, 73, 77, 78, 81; of life, 20, 21; peaceful, 71, 72; selection of, 13, 64–66
Pyramids, 80

Racine, Jean, 8
relationships, 11, 12
religion, vii, 5, 6, 7, 9, 25, 36, 42
responsabilité, 43, 44
response, 11, 43; signal-like, 18, 60, 62
responsibility, 7, 25, 35, 40, 42–45, 52, 64, 69; locus of, vi, 14, 65; toward nature, 15, 16; toward things, 16
responsorium, 43
Revue Internationale de Philosophie Moderne, v, xii, 2
Ricœur, Paul, ix, 2, 49, 64, 93
right-wing ideology, 33, 54
Rinrigaku, 15, 31
robots, 19, 59

St. Peter's Basilica, 29
Sakabe, Megumi, ix, 93
same-sex love, 22
schole, 8
science and technology, vi, ix, 3, 23, 26, 42, 43, 65, 66, 67, 68
science of cities, 2. See also *urbanica*
Sebastian, 43
self-alienation, 50, 62
self-control, 50
self-regulation, 10, 67–68
Sermon on the Mount, 41
sex, 6, 22, 35, 54, 70, 89, 90. See also intercourse
silence, 5, 21
silent phone calls, 26
sin, 29, 34, 56, 89, 92
sincerity, 40, 58

skills, viii, 28, 49, 58, 59
slaves, 3, 36; emancipation of, 3, 36, 42
smoke, 75–77, 83
social control, 18
social good, 67
social policies, 35
social violence, 34
socialist countries, 35
society, viii, 3, 6, 7, 8, 10, 29, 34, 45, 46, 50, 52, 57, 63, 67, 90; automobile, 18, 60; behaviour in, 21, 23; borderless, 2, 49; civil, 6, 16, 40; contemporary, 28, 42, 57, 59, 86, 87; and ethics, 1, 7, 9, 28, 35, 37; Japanese, 44, 45, 55; technological, 1, 2, 7, 8, 10, 23, 24, 26, 27, 30, 49, 67, 91; women in, 66
Socrates, 43
soundscape, 30
spatiality, 24, 50, 67
spirituality, 91
state, the, vi, 16, 20, 39, 48, 90
Stoic philosophers, 48
submission, non-autonomous, 18
supranatural, 91, 92
syllogism of action, 13, 14, 68
syphilis, 22

Takada, Saburō, 50
tapeinophrosune, 41
teaching devices, 59
Teachings of the Twelve Apostles, 41
teamwork, 85
technica, 2
techno-ethica, viii, 1
technological civilization, 21
technological innovation, 44
technological materials, 12
technology, 1, vi, 2, 5, 9, 12, 13, 21, 49, 52, 54, 58, 68, 71, 72; and culture, 8, 15, 26, 89; effect of, 22, 67, 85, 86; as part of our environment, 11, 18; and ethics, viii, 5, 23, 28, 55, 68; medical, 22, 68, 69, 73; and science, vi, ix, 3, 23, 26, 42, 43, 65, 66, 67, 68; self-regulation of, 67–68
technology-mediated environment, 1, 3, 10, 18, 21, 50, 58, 62, 68, 81, 83, 84, 89, 91, 92; advent of, 27, 58, 84; and changes in moral consciousness, vii, 21, 25, 30, 57, 58; characteristics of, 24, 86; definition of, 17, 82; effect of, 84, 85, 86; logical structure of action in, 63; and nature, vii, 82, 83, 84, 87, 88; and neighbours, vii, 51; origin of the concept of, 82; response to, 29, 60; and skills, 29, 58, 59; and time, 86, 87; virtues in, 46, 51, 52
telephone, vii, 12, 24, 51, 52. *See also* silent phone calls
television, 58
temporality, 8, 9, 50–51, 67, 86, 87
this world, 5, 60, 62, 64, 72, 73, 92
three houses across the road and the houses on each side, 23, 24, 25, 30
ties, 12, 36
time, vii, 8, 21, 34, 38, 46, 50, 51, 57, 60, 65, 67, 78, 85, 86, 87
Tokutomi, Roka, 75, 76
Toshimitsu, Isao, 93
totalitarianism, 18
treatment for sexually transmitted diseases, 22
treatment, medical, 22, 58, 63, 91
true nature of human beings, 90
Tsujimura, Kōichi, ix, 93

unethical, 29, 50
universalism, 36
urbanica, 2, 10

values, vii, viii, 5, 19, 21, 42, 44, 68
vending machines, 59, 62
Verantwortlichkeit, 44
Verantwortung, 43
virtue ethics. *See* aretology
virtues, vii, viii, 4, 5, 10, 26, 27, 28, 31, 33, 34, 36, 37, 39, 40, 42, 44, 45, 46, 49, 52, 58, 66, 85, 86; creation of, vi, vii, 10, 26, 28, 33, 34, 36, 37, 42, 44,

45, 46, 48, 49, 50, 51, 52, 58; history of creating, 34–37; new, vii, 10, 26, 28, 34, 36, 37, 42, 44, 45, 58. *See also* Aristotle, cardinal virtues of
volunteer, 63

wabi (reclusiveness), 44
waiting, ix, 87, 88, 89
Watsuji, Tetsurō, xii, 9, 11, 15
Watt, James, 43
Weltbürger (citizen of the world), 49
Weltwissenschaft (world science), 10

wisdom, 4, 33
wit, 50
work ethics, 46

Yamata no Orochi, 79
Yamato Takeru-no-mikoto, 19
Yata crow, 77

Zen, 63
Zengzi, 39
Zeus, 70
zum Brunn, Emilie, 93

www.ingramcontent.com/pod-product-compliance
Lightning Source LLC
Chambersburg PA
CBHW021132300426
44113CB00006B/390